I0455122

Understanding The Blush
Copyright: Raymond Crozier
Published: 2012

Publisher: www.raycrozier.com

ISBN-13: 978-1475106138

www.raycrozier.com

Contents

Introduction: What is a blush?

Colour and temperature provide common metaphors for our feelings. We say we are pink with embarrassment, green with envy and scarlet with indignation while blue is associated with sadness and depression, red with shame and yellow with cowardice. When we are frightened we go pale, tremble and feel the temperature drop, for example, 'my blood ran cold'; when we are angry we redden, our blood boils, we 'explode', 'blow our top' or 'blow a fuse', and we 'let off steam'. Blushing is described in terms of colour – 'I went red', 'she coloured', 'I turned beetroot', 'his cheeks were crimson' – and temperature: 'I'm burning up here', 'I felt my face burn', 'I was roasting', 'a warm shooting all over me'.

Blush is a very old word with its origin in the Anglo-Saxon word *ablisian* and its longevity suggests that it names an experience that has been widely shared for centuries. We find equivalent words together with their associations with colour and temperature in languages across the world, implying that the blush is a universal experience. For example, a fascinating international survey conducted by Michael J. Casimir and Michael Schnegg asked people across the world about the colours they associated with particular emotions.[7] Speakers of 135 languages and dialects were questioned and speakers of 98 of them made a connection between emotions and colour words: redness was associated with shame in 78 of the 98.

1

But what precisely is a blush? And why do we do it – what is it for? Does everybody blush, whatever their skin colour? Do some people do it more than others, women more than men, perhaps, or younger more than older people? Do children blush and, if so, at what age does this start – do infants blush? Often we find a blush charming or amusing, though perhaps more often in others than in ourselves, but for many people their blushing is a horrible experience, to be avoided if at all possible. Why should this be? These are some of the many questions that are raised when we reflect on the everyday phenomenon we call a blush and which I shall try to answer in this short publication. We don't have answers to some of these questions and many issues are controversial. Nevertheless we know much more about blushing than we did even 20 years ago and I aim to outline what we know – and admit what we don't.

Oxford Dictionaries Online defines the blush as 'a reddening of the face as a sign of shyness, embarrassment or shame' and this is similar to definitions in other dictionaries and in textbooks. Yet immediately this needs to be qualified. First, a blush involves more than reddening of the face and can involve the neck, ears and upper chest. Second, the definition excludes an important element, which is the experience of raised facial temperature and tingling experienced by the blusher, often the only way they are aware that they are blushing. Third, it assumes that there is only one kind of blush with the implication that the word maps onto a specific experience and presumably the physiology that underpins it. Finally, it asserts that the blush is associated with shyness, embarrassment and shame, and this too is controversial.

There is dispute whether the blush is specific to embarrassment and also whether it invariably accompanies it. Do we always blush when we are embarrassed or only on some occasions? Do we blush with other emotions too – shame, guilt or shyness – and does a blush always accompany these experiences? Psychologists recognise that there are differences among these emotional states so it is possible that there exists a particular psychological state that is common to all of them and it is this state that is associated with the blush. One candidate for this is the experience of heightened self-consciousness, which does accompany the blush and which is shared by these emotions; I write about this again in a later section.

An important contribution to our understanding of the blush in recent years has been the development of physiological measures which enable us to move beyond people's descriptions of their experience and their recollections of occasions when they blushed or when they observed others doing so. These measures can show whether the physiological changes correspond to the subjective experience; for example, they can determine whether people who are worried about their blushing redden as much as they think they do.

One technique in current use measures changes in blood flow in the blood vessels just below the skin by means of laser Doppler flowmetry. This involves illuminating a specific area of the face with laser light and collecting light that is reflected back onto a photo-detector. The measurement is based on a phenomenon known as the Doppler shift, which is the frequency change that light undergoes when reflected by a moving object, in this case, the flow of red blood cells. Increases in the measure correspond to increases in blood flow. An alternative approach records temperature at the surface of the skin, typically on the cheek or forehead. It seems from studies that use these measures that the blush is visible a short time before the blusher experiences the temperature change, implying that other people might notice our blush before we become aware of it ourselves. Future research may show whether this discrepancy in timing has psychological significance. No measure is a direct 'read out' of a blush; all devices have limitations and sources of inaccuracies and make assumptions about the relation between the blush and its measure, assumptions that may be unwarranted. For example the correlations between different measures that have been taken on the same occasion can be modest.

Is the blush a single phenomenon or is there more than one kind of blush? One of the earliest medical accounts of blushing – Harry Campbell's *Flushing and Morbid Blushing: Their Pathology and Treatment*, published in 1890 – attempted to identify different patterns of reddening in the face, but there has been little interest in continuing this work; perhaps this is because of what an

4

anonymous reviewer of Campbell's book in *The British Medical Journal* of 12th July 1890 called 'the inherent difficulty of the subject'. A blush is a fleeting phenomenon, difficult to capture for analysis. The psychologist Mark Leary and his colleagues distinguished between the 'classic' blush and the 'creeping' blush. The latter involves a slow spread of redness across the face, neck and upper chest region and is 'blotchy' in appearance; we often observe it when someone is performing in front of an audience, for example, giving a public presentation.[47] The classic blush is short-lived: In one study estimating its duration participants who were asked about their blushing reported it be of rapid onset (71% estimated that it came on within 2 seconds following the trigger) and of brief duration (average of 20 seconds).[64,] In comparison, the creeping blush has a delayed onset and can persist for several minutes.

Do these two patterns represent distinct phenomena with different mechanisms that happen to be called by the same name, presumably because there has been no need to distinguish them in everyday life? Or might the difference be an artefact of the different measurement devices, for example the measure of temperature might be slower to register a reading than the measure of blood flow? Perhaps the creeping version is simply a prolonged blush. In situations where the creeping blush is observed the individuals affected remain conscious of being the object of attention over a lengthy period and have no opportunity to escape their predicament. If they do not habituate to this exposure the blushing may not only persist but feed upon itself and spread across the whole blush region.

There is now some empirical evidence to show that the different blushes may correspond to psychophysiological differences. In a study reported by Marisol Voncken and Susan Bögels, participants undertook two tasks, giving a speech and initiating conversation with a stranger.[71] Their analysis showed a consistent increase in cheek *temperature* from baseline measurement taken prior to the task to measure taken during participation in the task, and the increase persisted after the task. In contrast, the measure of blood *flow* increased from baseline to participation in the task but dissipated quickly following the task. The redness associated with the persistence of higher cheek temperature might be what we observe in the creeping blush.

Peter Drummond and Hui Keow Lim reported that measures of cheek temperature and forehead blood flow taken during an embarrassing task were essentially uncorrelated.[27] They suggested that the fast-onset blush that is associated with increase in blood flow is instigated by neural mechanisms while the slower and more enduring change in cheek temperature is due to hormonal factors. Don Shearn and his colleagues also hypothesised that distinct mechanisms might be involved: the fast-onset blush reflects activity of the surface capillaries whereas temperature reflects activity of the venous plexus and 'deeper vascular structures'.[64]

Hopefully, future studies will confirm whether it is productive to postulate different kinds of flushes or blushes, for example by comparing physiological and psychological measures taken from the same participants when they encounter embarrassing predicaments as well as being involved in making presentations.

Physiology of the blush

The colour and heat metaphors for the blush suggest that it might be connected to thermoregulation, the system for regulating human body temperature. Thermoregulation involves processes such as shivering, sweating and the circulation of blood close to the skin, particularly in the face, hands, and feet, in order to adapt to changes in the environment and to maintain the temperature of the brain and the other principal internal organs at an optimal level. The mechanisms for thermoregulation involve an increase in blood flow close to the surface of the skin in order to cool the blood. Reddening of the face, along with perspiration and of course the subjective experience of heat, occurs in a hot environment, whenever we undertake physical exercise and following ingestion of substances such as alcohol and hot spicy food. Nevertheless, vasodilation of subcutaneous blood vessels causing increased blood flow occurs in reaction to other factors as well, for example, pressure on the skin or injury to it: Several mechanisms are involved in this range of vasodilation responses.

The anatomy of the blood vessels close to the skin in the blush region serves the process of body heat regulation and facilitates visible reddening of the face. There is a high density of blood vessels close to the surface of the skin and these are less obscured by tissue fluid than are vessels elsewhere. The system of skin blood vessels in the region has a distinctive structure. Blood flows along the arteries and resistance vessels (the smaller arteries and arterioles) in the subcutaneous layer into the capillaries in the epidermis; these form loops under the dermis before flowing through the venules into an extensive network of veins, the venous plexus. This network carries a large proportion of the volume of blood that flows close to the skin (it is the blood in the venous complex that produces coloration in people of paler complexion). The subcutaneous arteries have direct links to the venous plexus through vessels known as arteriovenous anastomoses, so that blood can be moved directly from arterioles to venules without passing through the capillary beds, thereby facilitating the flow of blood by reducing resistance. The arteriovenous anastomoses are controlled by action of the sympathetic nerves and, to a lesser extent, by circulating catecholamines [see below for an explanation of this term]. Thus the structure of subcutaneous vessels ensures that a substantial volume of blood can be moved quickly in order to regulate body temperature. In short, the area that we call the blush region has an anatomical structure that facilitates moving a large volume of blood close to the surface of the skin.[70]

It is plausible that the blush might involve the same mechanisms that produce the reddening observed in temperature regulation (for example, after physical exercise) since both entail vasodilation of blood vessels. In the process of thermoregulation the circulation of blood is under the control of centres in the hypothalamus. At normal body temperature blood vessels are maintained at a relatively weak base level of vasoconstriction by means of a degree of contraction of the smooth muscle within the wall of the blood vessels. Additional constriction or the relaxation of constriction is brought about by the transmission of signals from the hypothalamus along sympathetic adrenergic nerves. The neurotransmitter norepinephrine, which is released at the terminus of these nerves, binds to alpha-receptors in the muscle cells of the blood vessels to produce constriction. When temperature rises the hypothalamus sends signals to decrease sympathetic outflow in order to dilate the blood vessels. Therefore, vasodilation is produced by release of constriction produced by a decrease in sympathetic adrenergic activity.

In addition to neural activation there are several other causes of the constriction and dilation of blood vessels. These include the action of various hormones circulating in the bloodstream as well as local factors that originate either in the blood vessels themselves – endothelial or myogenic factors – or in metabolic and other activities in tissue surrounding the vessels – tissue factors. I look first at circulating hormones. Catecholamines,

9

including epinephrine (adrenaline) and epinephrine (noradrenaline), are hormones released by the medulla of the adrenal glands to circulate in the bloodstream. Circulating epinephrine binds to beta-adrenoceptors on small arteries and arterioles to cause vasodilation, a process that helps to prepare the body for fight or flight responses to threat.

Intrinsic factors include myogenic mechanisms that originate within the smooth muscle of blood vessels and substances that are synthesised in the endothelium (a thin layer of cells within the vessels) such as endothelial-derived nitric oxide. Finally, tissue factors cause vasodilation of blood vessels in various ways. Cells adjacent to the blood vessels release paracrine hormones such as bradykinin, histamine and prostaglandins. Bradykinin triggers the release of nitric oxide which has a powerful vasodilator effect; prostaglandins can be triggered by ingestion of the drug niacin [see below]. Adjacent cells release other substances which bring about localised vasodilation in various ways, by acting upon endothelial function or by stimulating the release of norepinephrine by the sympathetic nerves. Thus, although neural transmission of messages along sympathetic adrenergic nerves is regarded as the primary means of vasodilation of blood vessels in thermoregulation additional processes can cause dilation, and might contribute to blushing.

Nevertheless it is difficult to understand how the process of vasodilation involved in thermoregulation can account for the localisation of the blush. As far as we know, the visible reddening

10

and subjective experience of raised temperature are restricted to those areas we think of as the blush region. Recent research has begun to suggest that a rather different process of vasodilation of the facial veins may be responsible for generating a blush. Venous vessels also have vascular tone and the limited evidence that is available suggests that vasodilation in blushing may be primarily produced by activity of sympathetic nerves on the facial veins.

However, in the case of blushing it seems that it is not the action of sympathetic nerves upon alpha-receptors that reduces constriction; rather it is their action upon a different kind of receptor in the muscle cells of the blood vessels: the beta-receptors, which are found in the facial veins. A seminal study by Stefan Mellander and his colleagues examined the effects of drugs upon a section of human facial vein from the cheek region that had been removed for medical reasons during surgery.[52] They found that electrical stimulation of beta-adrenoceptors in the vein produced rapid vasodilation; furthermore, this effect was eliminated when a beta blocker drug was also administered. Research with intact veins and conscious participants undertaken by Margareta Nordin found that mental stress evoked bursts of sympathetic nerve activity in the supraorbital nerve (a branch of the frontal nerve which serves the forehead and scalp) which produced a vasodilator response and an increase in measured blood flow in the forehead region.[58]

An experimental study conducted by Peter Drummond confirmed the potential role of beta-adrenoceptors in blushing.[24] This study did not involve stimulation of an extracted vein, as Mellander's did, but the measurement of blood flow in a sample of participants who encountered embarrassing experiences such as failing to solve arithmetic problems and singing children's songs while making appropriate animal noises. Not surprisingly, participants reported finding these activities embarrassing. Measured blood flow increased during both activities but this was modified in conditions where drugs were administered to one side of the participant's forehead, drugs that were either agonistic (facilitative) or antagonistic to either alpha or beta receptors.

This design, which combines type of receptor with a drug that has either an agonistic or an antagonistic effect upon receptors, permits comparison of four conditions. One condition administered a drug that is agonistic to alpha receptors; a second condition applied a drug antagonistic to alpha receptors. A third condition applied a drug that is agonistic to beta receptors while a final condition administered a drug antagonistic to beta- receptors (specifically, propranolol, a beta blocker). It was found that the alpha-antagonist had no dilator effect, implying that alpha-receptors are not involved in blushing. On the other hand, beta-adrenoceptors seems to contribute to blushing, since administration of propranolol had the effect of reducing blood flow, albeit not completely. Evidently, beta-receptors are not the whole picture since there was some evidence of blushing even with their blockade.

Other factors have been considered as candidates for producing the blush including those causes of vasodilation described above: hormones that circulate in the blood stream, substances that are produced in the vascular endothelium of the blood vessels and in the surrounding tissues. The drug nicotinic acid (niacin) has been studied in the context of the prevention of cardiovascular disease since it has a strong vasodilator effect by releasing arachidonic acid, which in turn produces prostaglandins, increasing cutaneous blood flow and inducing flushing. This can be unpleasant for patients and a deterrent to their continuing use of the medication. Such findings have relevance for understanding blushing because of the observable effect of administration of the drug on cutaneous blood flow. The physiology of vasodilation of subcutaneous blood vessels and hence reddening of the face presents a complex picture that is not fully understood.

We have to take into account the possibility that a blush calls upon central or cortical processes. Although there exist rival theories of the causes of blushing all of them maintain that the blusher recognises at some level the psychological significance of the circumstances that evoke the blush. Whether this is recognition of a threat to your reputation or the awareness that you are the object of attention, some analysis of the meaning of the event is presumably required. The mechanisms are better understood in the case of fear where the role of the amygdala is central to the activation of the emotion (the amygdala is a set of sub-cortical nuclei deep in the temporal region of the brain). Sensory information about potentially threatening stimuli reaches the amygdala via stimulus recognition processes that are carried out in the sensory areas of the cortex and messages are sent from there to the amygdala to activate the emotional system. Nevertheless, we know that we often react to something before we know what it is and research has confirmed that conscious identification of a threat stimulus is not necessary to trigger a fear reaction.[59] Sub-cortical processes are sufficient when the processing of sensory information needs to be fast, enabling us to react urgently to a stimulus that might be dangerous, for example a sudden noise at night, a moving shadow, or a ball that seems to be approaching us at speed, before we fully appreciate what it is. Thus, we may react with freezing or with our 'hair standing on end' before we realise upon further analysis of the incoming information that it is insignificant and non-threatening.

As yet, we do not know whether equivalent sets of mechanisms are operative when we blush. Can it be triggered without conscious awareness of the nature of the threat? Sometimes we don't know that we are blushing, yet we might be aware of what it is that is its cause. Nor do we know whether there exist separate sympathetic nervous system pathways for different kinds of stimuli, for example for physical dangers and for threats to reputation.

14

As we have seen, reddening of the face is associated with emotions other than shyness, shame or embarrassment, for example, anger and indignation. Facial expressions as well as gestures and posture provide grounds for distinguishing between shame, shyness and embarrassment, on the one hand, and anger on the other. A blush is typically accompanied by an involuntary smile, eyes lowered, avoidance of eye contact whereas anger is expressed by raised and higher pitched voice, tension in mouth and jaw, and clenched fists.

Another cause of facial flushing that is accompanied by rapid temperature rise, palpitations and perspiration is associated with the menopause among women. Menopausal flushes are correlated with small increases in core body temperature within a range of temperatures where a woman does not shiver or perspire, and the frequency of menopausal flushes is related to climate conditions. For example, an international comparative study conducted by Lynnette Sievert and Erin Flanagan found that women reported fewer flushes in warmer temperatures, and the frequency of flushes is correlated with average annual temperature, difference between the warmest and coldest month in the year and the average temperature of the coldest month in the year.[66] This symptom can persist and cause distress, and research shows similarities between anxieties about hot flushes and the anxieties that can accompany blushing.[1] Cognitive behavioural treatments have been developed to help women cope with their flushes;

15

as I discuss in a later section, a similar approach has been taken to fear of blushing.

Why do we blush?

Darwin on the blush

Why we blush is a big question! Much contemporary science frames 'why' questions in evolutionary terms and the blush is no exception. Charles Darwin devoted a substantial chapter to the topic in his book *The Expression of Emotions in Man and Animals*, first published in 1872.[15] For many years this chapter provided the only extensive account of the phenomenon. It is still widely cited in books and articles on blushing and remains one of the most compelling accounts that we have. He collected information from correspondents all over the world, which led him to conclude that the blush is a universal phenomenon. Darwin reported that it is experienced by peoples whose dark skin complexion means that blushing is less visible. For example, he drew upon observations made by Thomas Burgess (in *The Physiology or Mechanism of Blushing* published in 1839) that a blush was visible on the scar tissue of a black woman and also that albino children born to black parents blushed.[5]

Darwin doubted that animals could blush and he argued that animals and human infants do not do so because they have not developed the necessary cognitive capacity. Only when we have developed the ability to represent in our own mind how we might appear to others, is a blush possible. These arguments are consistent with Darwin's thesis, set out on page 344 of his chapter, that it is 'the thinking of what others think of us which excites a blush':

> Whenever we know, or suppose, that others are depreciating our personal appearance, our attention is strongly drawn towards ourselves, more especially to our faces.

Darwin speculated that paying attention to one's face produces a blush because it directly induces vasodilation of blood vessels in the area attended to. Over the generations, he argued, this tendency would be strengthened through habit and would be passed on through inheritance. The face would be most likely to exhibit this tendency since it is our most conspicuous feature. This represents a Lamarckian explanation in that it calls upon the inheritance of acquired characteristics rather than regarding change as shaped by natural selection. Darwin saw little role for natural selection in the emergence of the blush as he claimed that it has no significance for adaptation to the environment.

This might be thought an unlikely position for Darwin to adopt, as elsewhere in his writings on the evolution of human characteristics he regarded adaptation as the key factor. In part this position may owe much to his reaction to the writings of Burgess on the blush and of Charles Bell, the anatomist and surgeon, whose *Essays on the Anatomy and Philosophy of Expression* on the expression of emotion more generally was published in 1824. Bell and Burgess were advocates of a 'design theology' explanation of emotional expressions, which regards them as designed by the creator to express specifically human moral feelings. Burgess assumed that the blush is specific to the human species because it was designed specifically to express conscience. As he wrote (pages 24-25),

> The Creator of man endowed him with this particular faculty of *exhibiting* his internal emotions, or more properly speaking, of the internal emotions exhibiting themselves, for no individual blushes voluntarily; it would, therefore, appear to serve as a check on the conscience, and prevent the moral faculties from being infringed upon, or deviating from the allotted path.

According to Burgess's conception of the blush, it would clearly serve a valuable social purpose as it would act to constrain conduct for the benefit of both society and the individual. This posed a dilemma for Darwin at a time when the theory of evolution was highly controversial and subject to attack on theological grounds. On the one hand, he accepted that the blush is unique to humans and that it is associated with shame, shyness and modesty, all emotions discussed by Burgess; on the other hand to propose that it evolved to fulfil a useful function for the individual and the species would bring him uncomfortably close to the theological explanation advocated by Burgess and Bell.

Darwin's attempt to resolve this dilemma illustrates distinctive characteristics of his explanation of the blush. First, he proposed that it is produced by self-attention acting directly on the vascular system. This explanation has received little attention, although recent research undertaken by Peter Drummond and Nadia Mirco has revisited it and yielded findings that are consistent with it.[28] They reported increased blood flow on the side of the forehead that is being scrutinised by an observer while the participant was taking part in an embarrassing activity; there was no change in blood flow on the other, non-scrutinised side. It is not unknown for attention processes to influence vasodilation and increase blood flow to specific parts of the body. Sexual arousal provides an obvious example, where imagination can be sufficient to induce increased blood flow to the penis and vagina.

Second, Darwin assumes that the capacity for self-attention requires a minimum level of cognitive development to have taken place. This is why the blush is unique to humans (and is not apparent in human infants, although we do not know when the blush first appears in childhood or what factors influence its emergence). Finally, Darwin emphasised that is thinking of what others think of our appearance that excites a blush. Our concern over what others think about our moral conduct represents an extension of this: 'the habit being thus acquired, would naturally be carried on when shame from strictly moral causes was felt' (p. 327).

The blush as a signal

Other theorists have framed evolutionary explanations of the blush in terms of its adaptive functions. One approach starts from recognition of the importance of communities and groups for survival. Social groups are found across living organisms, from ants and bees to chimpanzees and humans. They serve many functions. They can provide mutual protection and shelter and safety for raising and protecting the young, and they facilitate the sharing of essential activities. They make available a work force for large-scale tasks and provide opportunities for division of labour and the acquisition of specific expertise (in humans this has led from the construction of simple tools to the development of advanced technologies). Social organisation provides a base from which to explore and to extend habitats in order to maximise food supplies and to facilitate migration.

Groups can retain knowledge and skills and pass them on from one generation to the next. They establish rules and standards of behaviour to ensure their survival, and develop means for the regulation of conflict and aggression within the group. Their membership is differentiated in terms of role, status and power, which can be effective in resolving conflicts without the need for recourse to aggression that is costly for the group in many ways. Belonging to the group is vital for its members' well-being and social rejection can be serious, even fatal for members of many species.

Social interactions among members of groups have been studied extensively in primates, identifying dominance hierarchies and processes of affiliation, cooperation, competition and rejection. Human social interactions are clearly different from primates in many ways, not least because of our evolved capacity for language and the prevalence of symbol systems, yet it can be argued that equivalent processes are at work and that similarities in gesture and posture are often observed across species, for example in the display of submission. This perspective on the social life of humans provides one basis for understanding the blush. It may have originated as a sign of submission, and the gestures and posture that often accompany it – gaze aversion and lowered head – may display acknowledgement of low status and indicate a wish to abase oneself. It can also be interpreted as a sign of the individual's admission of wrongdoing and hence can serve as a nonverbal apology or wish to make amends. In short, it functions as a signal.

As we have seen, the *Oxford Dictionaries Online* defines the blush as a sign, something that communicates a message. Emotions convey information and the face is a primary site for this, in both humans and non-human species. Signals are common across the natural world. They are used to assert ownership of a territory, to claim possession of a mate or to indicate status within a dominance hierarchy. They display the individual's sexual

21

prowess, their sexual availability and readiness to mate. Signals are effective to the extent that they are 'honest' or sincere. They are said to be honest if, say, a signal of strength really does show that the individual is strong. The biologist John Maynard Smith provides the example of the roar of the Red Deer: the pitch of its roar is an index of its body size and is correlated with its reproductive success.[51] It makes sense for other deer to be impressed by the loud roar since it cannot be produced by a weak deer 'pretending' to be a strong one. An example of a dishonest signal would be a loud roar produced by an animal that turned out to be the cowardly lion in L. Frank Baum's *The Wonderful Wizard of Oz.*

The economist Robert Frank takes a similar approach to the analysis of emotions, recognising that the sincerity of signals is a crucial issue in human social encounters, particularly when the interests of protagonists are in conflict.[34] How do we know that an adversary is sincere and can be trusted? If an opponent displays a white flag of surrender how do I be sure that it is not a trap? If I am asked to lend money how confident am I that it will be repaid? Does he love me or is he only saying it to induce me to have sex with him? Frank argues that one guarantee of the sincerity of a signal is the difficulty of faking it. There are advantages in appearing honest and hence being trusted and a signal of honesty ought to be costly to fake: in the case of a blush, impossible to fake.

This is similar to the 'handicap principle', introduced by the biologist, Amotz Zahavi, which proposes that signals are guaranteed to be reliable when they are costly to produce.[72] It is always possible to present yourself as sincere while at the same time cheating to your advantage but while this might be beneficial in the short term it can prove costly in the long run as you risk losing your reputation as an honourable person, and this would result in being less likely be trusted in the future. By association, distrust might extend to people like you or to members of your family or a wider group to which you belong.

The blush has the potential to make a particularly effective signal since it cannot be feigned. We cannot control its onset or duration, whereas we can put on a false smile, mock anger or pretend surprise, and a verbal apology can be insincere but uttered with apparent genuineness. Cristiano Castelfranchi and Isabella Poggi have examined this issue in depth.[8] They argue that a blush does have a function and is goal directed: specifically it is a communicative signal of shame. They distinguish two forms of this emotion: 'shame before the self' and 'shame before the other'. I might feel shame before myself if I have cheated at an examination but nobody else knows this; or shame before the other if it is discovered that I cheated. If it looks plausible that I did cheat even if I know I had not done so, there would be shame before the other but not before the self. Castelfranchi and Poggi propose that a blush occurs when shame before the other is experienced, whether or not shame before the other is accompanied by shame before the self. In contrast, the blush does not accompany shame before the self if shame before the other is not present. Thus, if only I know I have cheated I will feel shame before myself but this shame will not evoke a blush. In the case of shame before the other, the blush has a goal, namely to inhibit a hostile response from others by indicating to them that I acknowledge wrongdoing (showing that I share the other's values) and regret my action. Although many interpretations of the blush have linked it with the experience of shame, Castelfranchi and Poggi are the first to make quite specific predictions about the nature of the connection and explain when shame does or does not lead to a blush.

Castelfranchi and Poggi add further conditions to the circumstances that trigger a blush in the case of shame before the other. The individual who blushes must have the goal of being positively evaluated by others with regard to our values: 'we can be ashamed only about things that cause, or may cause, a negative evaluation of ourselves' (p. 233). If the good opinion of particular others is not important to us, or we do not share a value about the behaviour in question, or we dispute the facts of the matter, we will not blush. Thus the value that is attached to cheating during examinations and the nature of those who have discovered my cheating will influence whether I feel shame before the other and will have reason to blush. The ultimate goal of the blush is to deter others from aggression towards me or rejection of me. The blush acknowledges the blusher's inferiority and assures others that I am not a threat to the group, whatever my conduct might have suggested.

The notion that the blush functions as a signal has attracted scientific investigation and several studies show that it can function in this way, for example a series of experiments conducted by Peter de Jong and his colleagues.[16, 17,18,20,21] Researchers present participants with short stories, 'vignettes', that portray scenarios of incidents, and they vary in a systematic way descriptions of the characters who are involved. They found that characters who have committed some misdemeanour are perceived more positively and their actions are judged to be less serious if they are described as blushing than if they are described as shamefaced or as showing no reaction. Characters who blush are also judged to be more likely to adhere to shared values than are those who are described as shamefaced or as simply leaving the scene.

These findings seem to suggest the communicative value of the blush in presenting the transgressor in a less negative light. It may do so by communicating the blusher's shame and embarrassment. Someone who is shamefaced after wrongdoing is viewed less negatively than someone with a neutral expression and even less negatively if a blush is also shown; adding a blush to a neutral expression also elicits a less negative judgment.[21]

Nevertheless, other empirical studies show that the interpretation of the blush depends on its context, in that observers take a negative view of blushers only in certain circumstances. de Jong and his colleagues extended their research design to investigate actual social encounters (as opposed to reports on vignettes) and to include a physiological measure of blushing.[19] Pairs of participants competed in a game (in technical terms, a 'prisoner's dilemma' game) where participants had the choice to either cooperate with their opponent or to play selfishly in each play of the game. Participants who adopted a selfish strategy blushed more (on the physiological measure) when they did so compare to when they cooperated. Their blushing was more likely to be noticed by their opponent. In addition, the more they blushed the less trustworthy their opponent judged them to be.

To summarise the implications of these studies: In certain circumstances, perhaps where there is no obvious intent to do wrong, you are regarded more favourably if you blush. In other circumstances, however, the blush is less advantageous and is likely to be interpreted as evidence of guilt or intention to do wrong. Clearly this interpretation often happens, and a blush may signify guilt even when the blusher is innocent. In one of my studies where I asked participants for personal recollections of occasions of blushing, one reported that, in a situation where many people were present and someone among them had committed a misdemeanour, she was thought to be the guilty party even though she was innocent, simply because she blushed.[10]

A further experiment by de Jong and his colleagues found that ambiguity about the intention of the actor seems to be a relevant factor in the interpretation of a blush.[18] If there was some ambiguity about whether or not an infringement was deliberate, the blush not only increased the likelihood that it would be judged as deliberate but also increased judgments of how serious it was thought to be. When the circumstances were not ambiguous about intent the blush had a more favourable influence upon judgments of intent and seriousness of the infringement; in these circumstances the blush seems to indicate remorse, or at least acknowledgement of wrongdoing.

It is important for these judgments of behaviour to be made that the blush is interpreted as such and not as something else. For example, if reddening of the face is thought to be induced by alcohol or seems to be a display of anger, a person's misdemeanour is not excused but is likely to be more harshly judged. While reddening of the face can be ambiguous about emotion other information can help to resolve the ambiguity, for example, evidence of the person's embarrassment or confusion, apologetic remarks, and so on.

In many circumstances the value of the blush may be that it conveys embarrassment in a convincing way. Rom Harré proposes a 'double ought' in embarrassment: there are occasions when in order to maintain a reputation for modesty you have not only to feel embarrassed but also to show that you are.[38] If you realise that you have inadvertently allowed your skirt to ride up or you are publicly congratulated on a recent success, you ought, as a modest person, to put matters right and show embarrassment. To give the impression that you don't care about your appearance or that you appear to find your success richly deserved would be immodest, shameless, perhaps conceited. You might *feel* embarrassed about the position in which you find yourself but if you wish to retain a reputation for modesty you also ought to *show* that you are embarrassed. This communicates to others your attentiveness to what would be considered to be a failure to meet standards of modesty and allows you to present yourself as of good character. Thus your embarrassment has to be visible; a blush is an effective way of making it so, and it is also convincing as it cannot be 'put on'. In Castelfranchi and Poggi's terms, the blush also indicates that you share the values of modesty even if on occasion you have not quite managed to uphold them.

However, it is not always the case that we want others to know we are embarrassed and often we prefer to hide our blushes. Presumably this is because we fear that embarrassment will create a poor impression and show us in a bad light, or because it may bring about even more embarrassment for us: we might be teased or mocked for our reaction, for example. We may fear that we have given ourselves away, revealing something that we wish to keep to ourselves, or we may appear guilty of something, whether or not this is the case. Embarrassment can often be a painful experience and this may be one reason why many people dislike and fear their blushing so intensely. Whereas a display of embarrassment shows others that we are aware of what is appropriate in the circumstances in which we find ourselves and that are conscious of our shortcomings it can give them the impression that we lack poise or sophistication.

Thus, it seems that there are some circumstances where a blush has desirable consequences and others in which the consequences are less helpful. An unusual example is provided by the novelist Henry Fielding in *The History of Tom Jones*, published in 1749. He portrays a 'Mrs Bridget' who had the advantage of being able to hear salacious gossip without compromising her reputation for innocence of such matters because she was able to 'conceal her blushes from the eyes of men'. As Fielding wrote (Chapter VIII), 'when a woman is not seen to blush, she doth not blush at all'. In this example failure to blush is interpreted as evidence of the character's innocence of the topic that is raised. Alternatively, as I suggested earlier, it might be interpreted as revealing someone's immodesty or shamelessness.

In summary, a blush can have positive outcomes for the person who blushes and for others who are present, and in the longer term for society as a whole. Even when it reveals the blusher's guilt and results in him or her being judged negatively, the blush can serve a useful function by bringing matters into the open and showing that the blusher acknowledges wrongdoing. As I have argued elsewhere, it helps everyone who is involved to cope with a predicament that has been created by the circumstances that cause one of them to blush and it enables the group as a whole to resolve any conflict that would arise and that would disrupt its activities.[12] Second, it adds to a group's cohesion by confirming that the errant member shares its values and thus belongs to it, and avoids the difficulties inherent in censuring or expelling one of its members. Finally, it strengthens the group through re-affirming its values and showing publicly that these are recognised and shared.

The thesis that the blush acts as a signal raises questions about the origins of the blush. In evolutionary terms how has it acquired this function? More specifically, does it serve as a signal among ethnic groups whose skin pigmentation renders the blush less visible and hence communication more problematic? One hypothesis about variation in skin colour traces it to the origins of *homo sapiens* in Africa some 200,000 years ago where the production of melanin was adaptive in providing protection from the sun's ultraviolet rays. Following migration to less sunny climates less melanin was necessary for protection and a lighter skin was adaptive in maximising the production of vitamin D from less ultraviolet radiation.

The implication is that lighter skin was determined by a genetic mutation that spread because it was advantageous to survival.[42] This raises the question whether the blush had evolved prior to this adaptation and, if so, how could it have evolved to serve a communicative function when all members of the species were dark skinned.

Evidence shows that the blush is found among peoples who have darker pigmentation and people

30

across the world are likely to associate the colour red with the experience of shame, with a tendency for those of darkest pigmentation to associate black with shame, influence by visible darkening of the skin associated with the blush.[7] There is evidence from a study of different ethnic groups in America that participants of darker complexion were more likely to refer to the experience of temperature change as evidence of their blushing and were less likely to refer to visible colour change.[67]

An experiment reported by Drummond and Lim compared male and female Caucasian and Indian participants on a mental arithmetic and a singing task that was potentially embarrassing.[27] They took measures of forehead blood flow and cheek temperature in addition to self-report ratings of self-consciousness, embarrassment and blushing propensity. All groups showed increases in cheek temperature and forehead blood flow during the embarrassing task but there were no differences associated with difference in skin tone. However, Caucasian participants believed that they blushed more intensely than Indian participants and reported greater self-consciousness and embarrassment during the singing task, even though the physiological measures showed a comparable increase in blushing in both groups.

The signal account assumes that communication is the primary reason for the blush but just because an expression has a signal function it does not necessarily mean that it evolved for this. For example, the pale face and trembling of fear are produced by the changes in the autonomic nervous

31

system that prepare the body for action. These reactions can have a communicative function, which may be useful when they alert others to our predicament and bring help but they can also be unwanted, as many people take the blush to be, when we do not wish to show fear, for example to an opponent in battle or, more mundanely in competitive sport. King Charles I of England is reputed to have requested an extra shirt at his execution in the winter of 1649 so that observers would not mistake his shivering in the cold for fear.

Theories of the signal value of a blush focus on its visibility and it is worth mentioning older accounts that also emphasise this aspect of the blush, but suggest that it serves as a mask to hide one's true feelings rather than as a means of displaying them. Michael Schoenfeldt quotes Lodowick Bryskett, who suggested in *A Discourse of Civil Life,* published in 1606, that blushing was caused by 'the minde finding that what is to be reprehended in us, cometh from abroade, it seeketh to hide the fault committed, and to avoid the reproach thereof, by setting that colour on our face as a maske to defend us withal'.[63] Similarly, Darwin (p. 320) quotes the fifth-century writer, Macrobius that 'nature being moved by shame spreads the blood before herself as a veil', as we see any one blushing often puts his hand before his face'. Shame is linked with covering up, hiding oneself or what one has done, and these explanations remind us of the apparent contradiction of the visible reddening and the impulse to hide that accompanies it.

Sex and the singular blush

The blush is frequently seen in a sexual context. Why should this be and might this tell us something significant about the origins of blushing? There are several possible explanations of the connection. An evolutionary explanation would relate it to sexual selection. Psychoanalysis would regard the blush as a symptom of unconscious sexual wishes. In theological terms, shame and sex are closely linked, for example in the Christian view of sexual pleasure (pudenda, the English word for the genitals, particularly women's, derives from the Latin word *pudere,* to be ashamed, specifically its gerundive *pudenda*, meaning things to be ashamed of. The less common English word pudency comes from the same source and means shame, bashfulness, and modesty). A social psychologist will observe that, in Western cultures at least, sexual matters are a frequent cause of embarrassment because they are regarded as a taboo topic that is uncomfortable to talk about. I look briefly at evolutionary and psychoanalytical perspectives before considering embarrassment in more detail.

Sexual selection

Survival of the group and of the species requires successful breeding and raising the young until they are old enough themselves to breed. In this way genes are passed on across the generations. The pattern of breeding contributes to the diversity of the population and the genetic composition of the population so that opportunities to adapt to changed circumstances are available to be taken. It benefits the group as well as individuals if they mate with members of the group who are likely to breed successfully, to have robust offspring, and to be able to protect their young while they are growing to adulthood.

There are various means by which individuals advertise their qualities to potential mates. In some cases they signal their availability for mating, for example in chimpanzees the rumps of females become swollen and bright red when they are sexually receptive. In other species males provide colourful displays to signal their positive qualities to prospective mates. The peacock's vivid display of tail plumes is a prime example of this and its effectiveness can be interpreted in terms of Zahavi's handicap principle.[72] The display demonstrates that the peacock is strong enough to survive despite its drawbacks, its weight and restriction on movement and the vulnerability to predators it creates. In evolutionary terms the benefits for reproductive success outweigh the costs.

Does the blush have a role to play in human sexual selection? Redness of the cheeks has long been regarded as a sexually attractive feature. For example, consider Matthew of Vendôme's description of Helen of Troy in *Ars Versificatoria*, written around 1175:

Her sparkling eyes rival the radiance of the stars,
And with engaging frankness play ambassadors of Venus.

With equal candour a blush that would make the captive
Rose pay tribute suffuses her face. As it fades away,
The blush proves no enemy to her face as rosy hue and
Snow-white skin contend in most delightful combat.

Shakespeare's *Romeo and Juliet* Romeo describes Juliet's beauty by admiring her eyes and the colour of her cheeks: 'The brightness of her cheek would shame those stars/ As daylight doth a lamp' (Act 2, Scene 2). The history of beauty in the face shows us that red cheeks have been found attractive for centuries. This is evident in painted portraits of beautiful women including portraits of the Virgin across the centuries, for example from Margarito of Arezzo's *Virgin and Child Enthroned*, of around 1262 to the nineteenth century Pre-Raphaelite Rossetti's *Fair Rosamund* of 1861 or the portraits of young women painted at the end of the nineteenth century and early twentieth century by Pierre Renoir or Amedeo Modigliani. You can see reproductions of all of these in Google Images.) The attractiveness of red cheeks was partly symbolic, as red was regarded as the colour of love, but it also reflects the perception of red cheeks as a sign of youth, good health and being in one's sexual prime. Red cheeks were associated with a fair complexion, 'snow-white skin' which was particularly valued in descriptions of women's beauty in medieval Western culture; white also had symbolic value, standing for purity. Cosmetics have long been applied to help convey the appearance of youth. There is historical evidence of the use of rouge in Egyptian, Assyrian, Greek and Roman cultures; for example, the Roman poet Ovid wrote about rouge in *The Art of Love* around the year 1 BC, 'You know the use of white to make you fair, And how, with red, lost Colour to repair.' Nowadays, as typing 'blush' into any Internet search engine reveals, cosmetics such as blusher are still applied to the face to increase a woman's attractiveness and give a youthful appearance.

Of course, a blush is not the same as a rosy cheek since it is a transitory change in facial colouring that accompanies emotion yet, historically the blush as a fleeting phenomenon has also been valued as a sexually attractive feature, particularly in women. Is the blush involved in sexual selection by heightening the blusher's sexual attraction to a potential mate, by providing a sign of the blusher's sexual interest or by indicating the blusher's acknowledgement that there is a sexual dimension to a particular social interaction? It is possible that there is something inherently blush-eliciting about sexual attraction. Alternatively, the association between the blush and sexual interest or attraction might be learned. The face conveys particular meanings within a given culture. In Western culture a particular colour arrangement is valued, although it might not have the same attraction in other cultures or at other times. To those who hold this value a blush will appear attractive, perhaps because it brings the face closer to the ideal white-and-red complexion.

A blush is an emotional response to particular circumstances and hence is revealing of the blusher's state of mind. This also might be a reason why it is sexually attractive. The blusher is temporarily confused, uncertain and vulnerable and this might make her more attractive to the other sex, at least in societies that have particular values about gender roles. One may think here of Charles Dickens' great novel, *David Copperfield*, where the eponymous hero is attracted to the vulnerable Dora; 'In the light room, Dora blushing looked so lovely, that I could not tear myself away'.

Psychoanalytical explanations

Sigmund Freud commented on the blush during a presentation by a fellow analyst Alfred Adler on a case study of compulsive blushing in 1909 (Bergmann provides an account of this session[2]). Freud argued that fear of blushing is due to unconscious shame; in the case of this patient, repressed shame of sexual knowledge and shame because of masturbation. He also observed that fear of blushing involved a conflict between two emotions, namely shame and rage.

There are several psychoanalytical perspectives on the blush but all emphasise its sexual basis in one way or another. Fred E. Karch offers an extensive overview of diverse approaches that have been taken, which have in common the basis of the blush in repressed sexual excitement.[43] Some accounts relate the blush to exhibitionism – the desire to be seen and be the object of attention, and conflict over this desire – the repressed wish to exhibit the genitals. Displacement of the sexual excitement from the genitals to the face occurs because of fear of castration. Psychoanalytical accounts also emphasise the place of shame in blushing, whether this is due to fear of castration or shaming of the child during superego development.

The accounts reviewed by Karch illustrate classical elements of psychoanalytical interpretation. This postulates the crucial role of unconscious sexual urges and fantasies underlying psychological phenomena. These can be traced to attempts to resolve the conflicts created by the (universal, according to Freud) Oedipal situation in early childhood, where the child sees his all-powerful father as rival for the love of his mother. It argues for the need for explanations of psychological phenomena to take into account defence mechanisms, where, in this case, the psychological meaning of the blush is displaced or disguised in some sense: for the meaning of redness in the face, look to the genitals. Interpretations of women's psychology often seem to be a variant of male psychology, as in accounts of fear of castration. For example, to quote Karch, reviewing the work of Feldman (p. 44),

> men blush because they fear being castrated, and women blush because they are not men' (p. 40) and 'two reasons for blushing in women: 1) to prove their innocence and chastity, and 2) to indicate sexual excitement and their interest in sex. In females, blushing is

rather simple but in males it is more
complex

Of course, psychoanalysis represents a rich set of concepts that have their meaning within a complex theoretical construction, and interpretation of an individual's behaviour is a complicated business; justice cannot be done to this in a couple of paragraphs. Nevertheless, the blush does not seem to have been the target of any greater attention within this framework than it has received within psychology more generally. Psychoanalysis places sexuality at the heart of the blush but, as we have seen, not in an obvious way.

Karch acknowledges that the attention it has received has been in terms of pathology and individuals who have anxieties about blushing rather than in terms of blushing in the general population. Nor is it obvious how these accounts can explain blushing in young children. Freud's own observations relate blushing to shame and rage and a conflict between them. Both emotions involve flushing of the face but the connection between them has not been investigated in the context of the blush.

As we noted earlier, there has been scarcely any research into blushing in childhood, in contrast to a large body of research into childhood shyness and, to a lesser degree, into embarrassment. Yet anecdotal evidence, informal observation and children's own accounts show that children do blush and become aware in early childhood of the circumstances where blushing typically occurs and its association with embarrassment. For example, a seven-year old boy gave me the following example of someone blushing, "Somebody tripped over when they were in a football match. They were embarrassed because I think they would be upset because they were doing so well and then they trip over."

In an interview reported by Stephanie Shields, Mary Mallory and Angela Simon, the most common response that participants gave to a question about the age at which they first recalled blushing was five years.[65] However, answers ranged from 3 to 23 years so it is quite difficult to interpret this information. Arnold Buss and his colleagues asked a sample of parents (mostly mothers) about any blushing or signs embarrassment in their young child[6]. Parents reported embarrassment in 21% of three-year-olds, 50% of five-year-olds and 72% of six-year-olds. According to the researchers, about half of these reports of embarrassment mentioned blushing, which implies that the blush can be seen in a minority of children from three years of age. (We know from extensive research into the development of children's sense of self that from around 22 months of age children show signs of embarrassment when viewing themselves in a mirror, when complimented, or when asked to dance in front of an audience.[48] But this research provides no direct information on blushing.) We need reliable data on children's actual blushing as opposed to recollections in order to understand when children first blush and why it occurs at a particular stage in development.

Is the blush inherently sexual or can the frequency with which it is associated with sexual matters be understood in cultural terms, reflecting society's attitudes to sexual activities, specifically that they are something to be hidden, to be ashamed of or to be embarrassed about? The implication of this would be that cultures with a more open or frank attitude to sex would be less likely to blush or at least would be less likely to do so because of this subject matter. Against this, one might cite Darwin's findings which suggest the universality of the blush and the tendency of sexual matters to trigger a blush in cultures across the world.

The anthropologist Andrew Strathern studied conceptions of shame among people in a mountainous region in Papua New Guinea, particularly their notion of *pipil* or 'shame upon the skin' that involves sensations of hot and cold on the skin and sweating.[69] When asked to describe circumstances when they experienced *pipil*, they gave examples of finding out that they have said something wrong when speaking in public, being seen urinating or defecating in public, being caught out having an adulterous relationship, or being found out breaking promises. What seems crucial is being seen, for example, one man said

> It is when people see us, it is not
> that there is anything inside it is
> outside only, it is when people see
> us doing these things that we feel

41

pipil, when they see our skin, and
we feel *pipil* on the skin.

Sexual and private bodily matters feature in the situations that trigger shame on the skin, but it is the public exposure of these rather than anything intrinsic to them that generates the experience of shame.

Do women blush more than men?

There is a common assumption that women are more likely to blush than men and that blushing is more attractive in women than in men, hence, perhaps, their more frequent use of cosmetics to produce red cheeks. Can we imagine Romeo refer to his blushing, as Juliet does when she says, 'Thou knowest the mask of night is on my face; /Else would a maiden blush bepaint my cheek/For that which thou hast heard me speak tonight' (*Romeo and Juliet,* Act 2, Scene 2). Would she find this characteristic attractive in Romeo? Why do we rarely talk of blushing grooms in comparison with blushing brides? Or are these questions of a sexist nature, influenced by cultural stereotypes about sex roles that are as outmoded as they are simplistic?

It would not be surprising if, at least in contemporary Western societies, women may be more self-conscious than men about their appearance, including their facial appearance. Conceptualising woman as the target of the male gaze is common currency in the social sciences.[32] Huge industries are devoted to marketing women's cosmetics and coiffure, to diet products and regimes, and to facial products and services from

42

anti-wrinkle creams, blusher, foundation, lipstick and mascara to Botox injections and cosmetic surgery. If, as Darwin proposed, it is 'the thinking what other people think about us which excites a blush', more self-consciousness about appearance would imply greater readiness to blush.

In fact, there does not seem to be much empirical evidence of significant gender differences in blushing. Bögels and Reith found that men obtained higher scores on a widely used self-report questionnaire measure of fear of blushing, trembling and sweating, but inspection of the separate components of the questionnaire revealed no gender differences including items on the frequency of blushing.[4] Amy Halberstadt and Laura Green also found no evidence of gender differences in blushing propensity (even though they did find that women had higher embarrassability scores than men, despite the fact that embarrassability correlated substantially with blushing propensity, r = .64).[37] In the interview study conducted by Shields and her colleagues with a sample of 65 more frequent and less frequent blushers identified no differences between men and women in their experience of blushing, consistent with other studies that report no gender differences.[65] They did find a statistically significant negative correlation between age and frequency of blushing; 64 per cent of participants aged 25 and under claimed to blush more than once a week; the figure was 28 per cent for those over 25. Individual participants also reported that they blushed less as they grew older.

Research incorporating physiological measures yields mixed findings. Don Shearn and his co-researchers found that, in comparison with male participants, women showed greater increases in cheek temperature while engaged in an embarrassing task and were judged to blush more by observers.[64]

On the other hand, there are studies that report no straightforward gender differences on physiological measures. For example, the experiment reported by Drummond and Lim, discussed above, with male and female Caucasian and Indian participants found no gender difference in increases in cheek temperature and forehead blood flow during an embarrassing task or an evaluative mental arithmetic task. Yet again, a study conducted by Marisol Voncken and Susan Bögels comparing a sample of patients diagnosed with social anxiety disorder with a control group, found no gender difference in measures of blood flow but there were differences in cheek temperature.[71] Men had higher cheek temperature overall, but women showed a greater increase than men in temperature when they began to give a presentation to an evaluative audience of two people or to interact with two others.

The inconsistent picture that research provides may be due to several factors. For example, questionnaire methods might be too insensitive to pick up gender differences. Physiological measures are difficult to interpret as the correlations between the various measures are modest and, as we have seen, they can point in different directions. The nature of the task has also to be taken into account, as giving a public presentation, being embarrassed, and completing a mental arithmetic task yield different findings. Studies have also involved different samples of participants, from clinical samples comprising individuals diagnosed with social anxiety disorder with and without blushing complaints to 'control' samples, which are often restricted to students within a narrow age range.

The kind of research that has been undertaken takes a rather crude approach that and pays insufficient attention to the situational nature of the blush. Simply to ask men and women how often they blush raises the question of what comparison they are making in order to answer the question. How often, compared to what or whom? Both men and women could believe that, say, women blush more than men do but at the same time both groups could answer realistically that they blush 'quite frequently'.

To discover whether a sample of women blushes more often than men we ought to take into account the relative frequency with which they encounter the kinds of situations that tend to trigger a blush. We would also consider the social factors influencing gender roles in these situations. For example, consider the possibility that women are more prone to blush at a sexually charged joke in mixed company, perhaps a sexual innuendo. The reason they might be more likely to blush could be due to cultural factors and expectancies that govern this kind of behaviour in a given society. One consequence of these factors could be that women

45

are less likely to hear such jokes in mixed company and hence would appear to be less likely to blush, a conclusion that fails to do justice to the complexity of the issue under investigation.

The other main sources of evidence – responses to vignettes and experimental designs – involve presenting participants with situations that tend to involve embarrassing predicaments where everyone is likely to blush and this might 'swamp' any gender differences. What seems to be a straightforward question is in practice difficult to address. At the very least, research has to sample a range of situations and understand something of the social norms and values governing them.

Embarrassment and the blush

What is the connection between the blush and embarrassment? As I have suggested, the blush is widely accepted as a sign of embarrassment although not all psychologists disagree with some disputing that it is specific to embarrassment and arguing that it is not a necessary component of the embarrassment display.[45] For example, research has used videotape and computer technology to provide a fine-grained analysis of the sequence of facial movements that occur when embarrassment is experienced, and this pattern does not necessarily include blushing.[44] A brief glance followed by looking away, involuntary smiling and attempts to suppress the smile, and touching or covering the face seem to be more fundamental to the expression of embarrassment than does reddening of the face. Yet there can be no doubt that blushing often goes along with embarrassment and sometimes the words are used interchangeably to describe emotional experience: 'you're making me blush' can mean much the same as 'you're embarrassing me'.

Blushing can refer to a group as well as to an individual, as the following sports headlines suggest: 'Rain spares England's blushes'; 'Red-faced England held at home'. These surely refer to the embarrassment that has been caused, in these examples by unexpected failure, rather than widespread blushing among the population. More generally, the circumstances that evoke a blush are similar to those that elicit embarrassment and an inventory of situations that make people blush would resemble a list of embarrassing episodes. Finally, research conducted by psychologists contrives embarrassing predicaments in order to elicit a blush for study.

Embarrassment is triggered when some circumstances, whether externally generated or brought about by the embarrassed individual's own actions, create a predicament for the individual and perhaps also for others who are present. The predicament threatens the individual's social identity and makes it difficult to maintain a desired impression. It makes it difficult to know how to proceed, to continue playing a part in the social encounter. The embarrassed person can be flustered and at a loss for words.

There exist several theories of embarrassment and attempts to classify embarrassing circumstances. John Sabini and his co-authors offer one classification of the circumstances, proposing these can be subsumed under three types of events: committing a *faux pas* in front of other people; being the centre of attention for reasons other than making a *faux pas*; doing something to threaten the identity of someone else present.[61] Examples of these are, respectively, being dressed inappropriately for an occasion; entering a busy room and everyone turns to look at you; asking someone to return money they have borrowed but not paid back.

This analysis closely resembles a classification of blushing circumstances offered by Leary and his colleagues: threats to public identity, such as violations of social norms, inept performances, loss of control, and behaving out of role; receiving praise and positive attention; being the object of attention; being accused of blushing.[47] The kinds of circumstances that lead to a blush can be assigned to these categories and represent embarrassing predicaments. You arrive late for, say, a meeting when everyone is already seated, and you blush as you try to find a seat. In the supermarket your child makes a loud remark about the appearance of another shopper. Your boss praises you for the extra effort you have put in. And, of course there are all those embarrassing mishaps and *faux pas* that are the staple of comedy: soup is accidentally spilt on a dress or the wrong cutlery is picked up; you realise when you arrive at the party that it is not the fancy dress occasion that you have prepared for; you ask a question in front of the class which the tutor has only just answered for another student;

Ailis realises that she is expected to introduce Betsan to Cara but she has momentarily forgotten Betsan's name. Threats to social identity, encountering obstacles to making a desired self-presentation, being flustered and being the object of attention are common causes and accompaniments of both embarrassment and blushing, although threatening another's identity has not been studied in the context of blushing. Accusing someone of blushing can cause them to blush; it is not clear whether accusing them of being embarrassed would make them embarrassed or cause them to blush, but it seems plausible that this can happen.

Robert Edelmann proposed that blushing can lead to embarrassment in the absence of any specific predicament and feedback from your blushing can be the trigger for you to label your experience as embarrassment.[29] Some people who are anxious about their blushing do say that they blush in situations where they do not feel embarrassed, although the awareness that they are blushing creates social difficulties for them as they imagine what others will think of their visible reddening. Edelmann emphasises the importance of the individual's cognitive appraisals in this process; as we shall see, interventions to help people with concerns about their blushing can target these appraisals with the aim of changing how they imagine others interpret their reddening.

Within this overall picture a large number of different kinds of events can produce embarrassment.[53] The picture is complicated when we take into account circumstances where the

49

embarrassed individual is an observer of the situation rather than actively involved in it, for example listening to an inept performance by a singer or musician, or attending a comedy show where a comedian is struggling to amuse the audience. You can experience vicarious or empathic embarrassment, be embarrassed by or for someone. You can be embarrassed by overhearing others engaged in sexual intercourse or arguing furiously in an adjacent room, particularly if you know them well or have to meet them again the next morning.

In such circumstances it is difficult to see how the emotion is produced by loss of esteem in either one's own eyes or the eyes of others or even understand how it creates a predicament, particularly when the observer is remote from the action, for example when watching a performance on television or as an anonymous member of a large audience. I was recently in the audience for a play in London, and soon after it started a naked actor strolled on to the stage to join a group of (clothed) actresses; the audience's initial surprise was followed by widespread embarrassment that was palpable. Embarrassing circumstances and predicaments induce laughter. Smiling and attempts to control a smile are also classic elements of the embarrassment display.

That sexual matters can be embarrassing can be understood in terms of current psychological theories. For example, unintended nakedness is a common source of embarrassment. This can be elicited by actual exposure, which is often linked with mishaps, making *faux pas,* losing bodily control and so on, circumstances that are sufficient in themselves to produce embarrassment. Inadvertent exposure is frequently mentioned in surveys as a cause of embarrassment and this has been categorised by psychologists in various ways, as loss of control over one's possessions, as producing a situation with inappropriate sexual connotations or as a breach of privacy.[12]

It can also be elicited when the exposure is less direct, for example when you recall a previous experience or when you suddenly realise that you have been exposed on an earlier occasion. Talk about exposure can trigger a blush, for example in a conversation when someone mentions genitals, or menstruation or toileting. Observing someone making blatant sexual advances or listening to someone recounting their sexual experiences can also be embarrassing. Consider an example from Laurence Sterne's novel, *The Life and Opinions of Tristram Shandy, Gentleman*, written between 1759 and 1769 (volume IX, chapter XX, pages 71-74; I have simplified the punctuation). In this episode a 'Mrs Wadman' believes that 'uncle Toby' is offering to show her an injury he has received in the genital region.

> "You shall see the very place, /Madam," said my uncle Toby.
>
> Mrs Wadman blush'd, look'd towards the door, turned pale, blush'd slightly again, recovered her natural colour/blush'd worse than

51

ever; which for the sake of the unlearned reader, I translate thus, "L..d! L..d! I cannot look at it, What would the world say if I look'd at it? I should drop down, if I look'd at it, I wish I could look at it, There can be no sin in looking at it, I will look at it."

It is interesting that Sterne describes his character's immediate concern is in terms of the taboo against looking at what should be kept hidden followed by concern with what other people would think of her if she did break the taboo, looking towards the door as if someone might observe her doing so. In Castelfranchi and Poggi's terms this would be shame before the other and it is consistent with theories of the blush that emphasise the salience of the blusher's concern with how he or she will look to others. She blushes yet again but more intensely this time while she keeps the forbidden topic in mind, as Sterne describes the conflict she experiences between the urge to look and not to look.

Yet there are many instances of exposure that give rise to a blush which are not obviously sexual or to do with the body. For example, a blush can be elicited when a sensitive or personal topic is raised during a conversation, someone guesses a secret you wish to keep or uncovers your motives for your action; in these circumstances you may redden whether or not you had been the centre of attention. What these circumstances share, along with many other triggers of blushing, is the exposure of something that you believe ought not to be exposed in this situation. My own thoughts on this, which I have discussed at greater length elsewhere are that exposure or its anticipation is fundamental to blushing.[10,11,12] Specifically, if an event X brings, or threatens to bring into the open a topic Y, and Y is something the individual believes ought to be kept hidden in these circumstances, X will elicit a blush.

A sense of exposure can be triggered simply by a shift in your awareness, by bringing something to mind. You suddenly suspect that you are the centre of attention; or you become conscious of how what you are doing might be interpreted by others. A literary illustration of how subtle such a change can be can be found in George Eliot's novel, *Daniel Deronda*, first published in 1876. Eliot writes of her character: 'some consciousness arrested her, and involuntarily she turned her eyes towards Deronda...He, like others, happened to be looking at her, and their eyes met – to her intense vexation, for it seemed to her that by looking at him she had betrayed the reference of her thoughts, and she felt herself blushing'. Just a shift in her consciousness is sufficient and the coincidence of their eyes meeting gives her the impression that her private thoughts have been exposed. It is the (imagined) fact of their exposure, not necessarily what the thoughts are about, that triggers the blush. The choice of the word 'betrayed' implies that the thoughts ought to have been kept private for whatever reason; their revelation is a breach of confidence.

We can think of this in terms of the distinction between a private self and a public self. We can trace the antecedents of this idea to the seminal book *The Principles of Psychology*, published in 1890 by the philosopher William James. He had a profound influence on thinking about the self, in his distinction between *I* and *Me* and the notion that we have more than one self. The I-self is the self as knower, and the Me-self is the self as known, it is what I have in mind when I reflect upon myself, worry about myself, wonder what others make of me. James also argued (page 294) that 'a man has as many social selves as there are individuals who recognize him and carry an image of him in their mind' and this notion of the multiplicity of the self has been very influential in social psychology. If the public self or selves are what we present to the world and represent the image we create in others, the private self or selves represent those aspects of the self that we would not necessarily want others to know, or at least not want some others in some situations to know. There are also matters that are not necessarily personal that we would not want to be associated with. In these terms, exposure may be the potential 'outing' of the private self.

Exposure has consequences for the individual, or at least he or she believes that it does: I ought not to be seen in this position; others will think less of me if they find this out; the time is not right to reveal this; this will make it awkward for someone else; you have caught me out; I will find it difficult to cope with the situation this disclosure will create.

The fact that you blush can, in many circumstances, have implications for how you are judged by others. A blush can be a signal to others that you do share the value that a particular topic ought to be hidden and this will tell them something about the kind of person you are (of course you might not want to convey this particular impression, in which case the blush is unwanted). Failure to blush can signal that you do not adhere to the value (if the value is widely held you may be thought shameless, brazen or unblushing). A woman hearing a lewd remark in mixed company ought to blush, as should a man hearing another man make a sexist comment in a woman's presence.

On the other hand, if you do not recognise that a particular topic ought to remain covered for whatever reason, you have no reason to blush when it is brought to light. The context of the blush is clearly important. Raising the same topic will induce a blush in one situation but not in another, will cause one person to blush but not another. Simply bringing a topic into the open is not sufficient to elicit a blush. What is also necessary is that the topic uncovers something. The suggestion here is that whether one blushes or not is related to the distinction between exposure and conspicuousness. In the first case something hidden is uncovered, and to assert this is to claim more than saying that something is made visible.

We can extend this to take account of occasions when people go red when they are praised or thanked. These occasions bring our achievements into the open in a way that is inconsistent with standards of modesty. To blush at a compliment is to suggest unworthiness of it and to show yourself as modest. Such occasions can also create a predicament as it may be difficult for you to respond with the appropriate degree of modesty, particularly under the spotlight of public attention, and they take you out of your 'comfort zone'. The private self becomes public. Consider the example of people watching television who are suddenly presented with an explicit sexual scene. Under what circumstances will they blush? Most writers on blushing would assume that viewers would not blush if they were watching on their own. We might hypothesise that they would be less likely to blush if they were viewing in the company of someone who holds similar attitudes to themselves on the content of the programme. On the other hand, they would be more likely to do so if they were in company and personally regarded the topic as taboo, or if they were comfortable with the topic but had reason to believe that fellow viewers would find it a taboo topic (for example, someone of a different generation) or if they were uncertain about other viewers' attitude. Some kinds of topics seem to be more likely to be regarded as properly hidden in a given society at a given time; nevertheless the immediate social context has to be taken into account in order to predict who will blush and when.

This hypothesis encourages speculation about possible factors in the evolution of the blush, which might be a response to physical exposure that has become extended to psychological exposure. Being exposed to view is potentially dangerous for any organism as it makes them vulnerable to the attention of predators, and many species develop mechanisms to enable them to remain hidden or disguised as they move about their environment, for example camouflage. Freezing and playing possum are other anti-predator responses, as either an involuntary reflex or an active defensive strategy.

Inhibition of ongoing action is a common fear response. It is conceivable that the blush is a physiological response associated with the interruption of activity due to sudden exposure to potential threat. The psychologist Nico Frijda argued that 'in all instances of blushing, then, there seems to be an action tendency that is stopped, blocked, or suppressed.[35] Blushing thus could be a response of sudden inhibition of some tendency to act' (p. 168), an inhibitory response that counteracts 'conspicuousness hazards' such as social criticism or making *faux pas*. Eric Salzen suggested how this might take the form of a vasodilation induced blush.[62] Blushing occurs when the immediate impulse when you find yourself the centre of attention - to escape attention - is not possible and the escape response is inhibited. This is a 'physiological rebound' where the flow of blood towards the musculature in order to initiate action is interrupted.

Anxiety about blushing

Despite its potential advantages for deflecting criticism or rejection blushing is an unpleasant experience for many people and can be a source of great anxiety. Blushing resembles embarrassment in this respect: both can be painful experiences which most of us steer clear of as much as we can, even if this can only be achieved by behaving in a very defensive way or by avoiding situations which we anticipate will cause us distress. Fear of embarrassment can have a profound influence on individuals and have serious implications for society. People may put off vital medical examinations or be reluctant to contribute to sex education because of their embarrassment.

Lack of exercise leading to obesity can in many cases be traced to self-consciousness about our bodies, for example research shows that embarrassment is a factor in the declining rates of participation in sports among young people, particularly girls. Embarrassment can be about communal showers, being obliged to wear revealing and unflattering apparel and about the teasing and harassment that can accompany physical exercise classes shared with boys.[9] These create particular problems for those who are shy or sensitive about their appearance or who hold certain religious beliefs. For example, being seen in sportswear could be unacceptable to Muslims who practise pardah or who comply with strictures against participation in activities in ways that attract the male gaze.[32]

Blushing, and the circumstances that give rise to it, can also be a source of embarrassment and discomfort for most of us. Yet for many individuals their anxieties about blushing cause serious problems in their everyday life. They feel uncomfortable when they are in company because they don't know when they might suddenly redden. A blush is difficult – perhaps impossible – to prevent or to control once it has started. Anxieties are heightened not only by the awareness that blushing is uncontrollable but also because simply thinking about blushing can induce it or intensify it once it has started. Like many fears, something that starts off as a minor inconvenience can come to loom large in your life.

Anxieties about participation in social interactions and occasions are very common in contemporary society. Most of us feel shy or lack confidence in at least some of the situations we encounter. We can put some figures to 'many' and 'most'. Surveys of shyness in the general population find that over 40 per cent describe themselves as shy people, and over 60 per cent of those who consider themselves to be shy regard their shyness as a problem.[40] This research draws upon people's common sense notion of shyness.

Other studies have investigated the prevalence of the clinical condition of social phobia (increasingly 'social anxiety disorder' is replacing this term), an anxiety disorder characterised by a persistent fear of social situations that has a significant impact upon the person's life. The individual diagnosed with this disorder is likely to feel self-conscious in company, find everyday social encounters difficult to deal with and fear being criticised and rejected. As the support group Social Anxiety UK states on its web site, 'sufferers typically experience feelings of nervousness or dread in relation to feared social situations. They may experience specific physical symptoms such as trembling, rapid breathing, sweating or blushing. At the extreme, panic attacks can occur '. [68]

Social anxiety disorder is the third most common anxiety disorder (after depression and alcohol dependence) and data suggest that more than in ten people will meet the criteria for diagnosing the condition at some time in their life.[56] The internet based charity No Panic estimates that up to one million people in Britain suffer from the disorder.[57]

There is a clear connection between social anxiety and anxiety about blushing. One survey found that a substantial proportion of a sample of people who actively sought information about surgical treatment for their blushing (see below) met the diagnostic criteria for social anxiety disorder: 60 per cent of those reporting blushing concerns and 54 per cent of those reporting blushing and sweating concerned met the diagnostic criteria.[36] Research also shows that people who meet diagnostic criteria for social anxiety disorder are more likely to report concerns about blushing than are patients with other anxiety disorders. Thus, Fahlén has shown that concerns about blushing are reported much more frequently by patients with social anxiety disorder than they are reported by patients diagnosed with other anxiety conditions.[31] There is evidence too that individuals with generalised social anxiety disorder report more problems with blushing than do those with the non-generalised type.[31] (The generalised type is where people persistently fear a variety of social situations, not merely specific kinds of situations such as speaking up in front of a group or asking someone for a date.) Finally, the study showed that among those meeting diagnostic criteria for social anxiety disorder, blushing was rated as more intense a problem than other physiological symptoms of anxiety, with 25 of the 63 participants assigning it the highest possible intensity rating.

Yet many people who are anxious about their blushing regard this as the basic cause of their problems. They do not think of themselves necessarily as shy or as socially anxious, rather they believe that if they did not blush so often or so visibly they would not experience the social difficulties that they do. They report blushing even when they are not shy or embarrassed. In their view, their blushing is not a sign or symptom of an underlying shyness or anxiety; it is a problem in its own right, with the implication that if the blushing could be eradicated their social difficulties would disappear.

These beliefs raise questions about the nature of concerns about blushing. What is it about it that is so disturbing? Do those who experience these anxieties blush more frequently, more intensely or more visibly than other people do? Could they learn to think about their blushing differently, in a more positive way or at least in a more accepting and relaxed way? Is it the case that blushing can be separated from anxiety about blushing so that its eradication would minimise anxiety? Or is attributing difficulties in social situations to the blush mistaking the symptom for the underlying anxiety of which it is a symptom, a misattribution that can easily be made because the blush is so visible and vivid?

These questions have implications for helping people overcome their anxieties. If the problem is primarily one of anxiety then attempts to help (interventions or treatments) should focus on anxiety. If it is primarily one of reddening then blushing itself should be the focus of intervention. As I discuss below, treatments of fear of blushing (a technical term is erythrophobia) either focus on anxiety (psychological therapies or anti-anxiety medication) or on the blush (surgical intervention in the form of endoscopic thoracic sympathectomy).

Problems with blushing

The anxieties that are described by people who have problems with blushing and the fears that are expressed about the consequences of blushing are essentially social ones, similar to the fears and anxieties described by people diagnosed with social phobia who do not identify blushing as their primary concern. You worry about what others will think. You believe that they will think less of you or will reject you because of your reddening. Your blushing will attract attention and reveal that you are not comfortable or in control of the situation. Others may take your blush as evidence that you are silly, nervous or immature. People comment on your redness, perhaps taunt or tease you about it, and this makes you feel bad. You believe that your blushing is extreme or disproportionate to the situation. You anticipate going red and are aware that anticipation in itself is likely to make you blush.

Blushing often coincides with fluster and confusion, being inhibited and tongue-tied, and this too becomes cause for anxiety as it undermines the desired image of poise and being in control. At the heart of it is the fear that others will see you turn red; if you did blush but this was not noticeable then it would not be a problem. Implicit in this is the belief that being seen to go red is a bad thing, presumably because of what others will think of you as a consequence. Accordingly, your blushing makes you feel bad about yourself and you feel depressed. There is a vicious circle here: you blush because of anxiety and you are anxious because of your blushing.

The fear spreads beyond blushing to become anxiety about social situations, at least those where it is important for you to make a good impression on others or to avoid making a poor impression, such as dating, speaking up in front of others, or making a public presentation, and dealing with authority figures. (These are also the kinds of situations where people in general say they are most likely to be shy, and which shy individuals find the most problematic; they are not specific to blushing anxieties.) Avoiding these kinds of situations only serves to maintain the anxiety since they deny you the opportunities to learn that the situation is not as you fear it to be.

The descriptions of their anxieties given by individuals who are worried about their blushing are replete with descriptions of anxiety about social situations and fear of what others will think. Their accounts reflect assumptions about how their blushing is perceived and interpreted by others and about what others will think of them as individuals in consequence. Such beliefs are regularly encountered by psychological therapists and counsellors when they discuss anxieties and phobias with their patients or clients. This suggests that treatments for fear of blushing ought to focus on bringing into the open the blusher's perceptions and beliefs in order to discuss, analyse and change them.

Those who experience these anxieties believe that their blushing is extreme or disproportionate in some way. Is there any evidence that they might exaggerate the extent of their blushing, that in reality they blush less than they think they do, and that they do not necessarily blush more than others would do in comparable situations? Research to address this question needs some objective measure of blushing to compare with the blusher's subjective experience and with observers' perceptions of the blusher. Recent advances in the measurement of blushing permit this and we are beginning to collect some relevant evidence.

Sandra Mulkens and her colleagues found little evidence that beliefs about one's own blushing were correlated with physiological measures of blushing when the participants in her study were engaged in an embarrassing task; self-reported blushing was not correlated with ratings of their blushing made by observers of their behaviour or with physiological measures of cheek coloration or facial temperature.[54] Participants who obtained high scores on a questionnaire measure of their tendency to blush reported that they blushed more than others in the task situation even though neither the physiological data nor the reports of observers showed that they did actually blush more.

The differences obtained between blushers and non-blushers were not found on physiological measures, only in beliefs about their blushing. The only physiological difference that the researchers identified was when high scorers on the blushing questionnaire were provided with feedback that they were blushing: this feedback was associated with a measurable increase in blood flow in this group.

Yet the picture is more complex and there is evidence that the greater anxiety about blushing is not necessarily due to mistaken beliefs about blushing; there are also some differences on physiological measures between individuals who are more anxious about their blushing and those who are less so. A blush may be more likely to persist among people who are anxious about their blushing. Drummond and his co-researchers found that participants who reported high blushing

65

anxiety did not differ from those low in anxiety on measures of increased blood flow at the beginning of an embarrassing task but the increase in blood flow persisted longer among the high anxiety group.[54]

A separate study distinguished two groups of people diagnosed with social anxiety disorder: those who also have blushing complaints and a second group that do not. [71] Participants undertook two tasks, giving a presentation and having a conversation with someone they didn't know. The two groups differed not only on self-reports of their experience but also on a physiological measure of cheek temperature. They also differed when the effect of participating in the social tasks (the presentation and the social encounter) was analysed. There was no effect of task on the measure of cheek temperature but there was an increase in blood flow when the social task began and a decrease when it ended, and both the increase and the decrease were greater among participants who were anxious about their blushing than they were among those who were not anxious.

Fear of blushing may be due to beliefs about the consequences of blushing rather than about its frequency, that those who hold such beliefs may exaggerate the seriousness with which others take the blush or have an over-pessimistic view of the interpretations that others place upon it. This was addressed in a study reported by Peter de Jong and Madelon Peters.[17] They presented two groups of participants who differed in blushing anxiety with vignettes describing the outcomes of transgressions and mishaps; in half of the vignettes the 'actors' were described as blushing. Participants rated the extent to which they believed observers of the actor would perceive the actor and the situation.

Overall, the high-anxious group gave higher ratings than the less anxious group on items referring to whether observers would interpret the events as intentional, would see the situation as more serious and would regard the actor as less reliable. However, the reference to the actor's blushing had no influence on the ratings of either group.

The pattern of results suggested the cognitive bias that is characteristic of people who are highly anxious: people are likely to view you negatively in such circumstances. However, it failed to show that specific concerns about blushing influenced their beliefs about such outcomes.

Studies like this one tend to present vignettes that involve predicaments where perhaps most of us would blush (we saw this limitation in the case of studies of gender differences). Perhaps people who are highly anxious about blushing are concerned that they will redden in situations where others would be unlikely to do so. In order to investigate this possibility, Corine Dijk and her colleagues examined beliefs about blushing in a range of situations where the blush would not necessarily be expected.[20] This study too compared groups high and low in self-reported fear of blushing (they were recruited from an Internet forum devoted to blushing concerns). It found that high-fearful participants anticipated being more likely to blush and being judged more negatively when they did blush in a range of everyday situations. They perceived themselves to be 'weak' and 'strange' when they blushed.

Again, as is the case for studies of gender differences, sampling a wider range of situations is necessary to bring out the beliefs that anxious people have about social situations in general and about the consequences of specific situations. Anxiety about blushing is associated with negative beliefs about the blushing self: I am weak, odd, less socially competent than others.

Treatments for anxiety

Cognitive behaviour therapy

People who are anxious about their blushing often adopt what cognitive behaviour therapists call 'safety behaviours', strategies that are intended to minimise the visibility of their blush. These range from applying cosmetics, adopting hairstyles or wearing clothes that cover as much of the face and neck area as possible, to keeping in the background and even avoiding situations that are likely to trigger a blush. Safety behaviours are typically counter-productive. Their focus on the self heightens feelings of self-consciousness, which are more likely to instigate a blush. They encourage anticipation of blushing which also makes it more likely to occur.

Whatever short term respite these behaviours appear to offer they deny the anxious person the opportunity to change, to realise that others hardly ever notice their blush and rarely make anything of it, that any teasing is soon over, may be good natured and are evidence of warm feelings towards the blusher, and has no lasting effect.

Cognitive behaviour therapy rests on several assumptions. Behaviour patterns can be changed and even long-term entrenched anxiety can be reduced. Behaviour is maintained by a set of beliefs and these must be brought into the open and challenged. Defensive safety behaviours should be understood for what they are and be replaced by more productive strategies. Change requires putting new behaviours into practice during therapy sessions and in 'homework' assignments in real social situations: the process involves activity and reflection upon activity, not simply talk.

The cognitive approach focuses on challenging negative beliefs about blushing and its consequences. It encourages the anxious person to analyse the contents of statements that they repeatedly say to themselves such as 'everyone notices my blush' or 'blushing makes me look silly'. Therapists understand that safety behaviours and avoidance strategies are entrenched and resistant to change, and that the process of change involves systematic and gradual exposure to the kinds of situations that the individual fears.

Participants engage in behavioural experiments, in role play during sessions or in actual social situations, where they systematically try out strategies and assess what effects these have. For example, the participant might be asked to go into company with blush-hiding cosmetics and then interact with people without them, or to swap their turtleneck sweater for a round-neck to see if people respond to them differently. Or they might emphasise their blush by using blusher cosmetic and then go into social situations to see if their blush is noticed.[60]

Participants are encouraged to practise closely observing others' reactions rather than make assumptions about how they would react. Of course, if you are anxious about blushing these tasks will be very difficult and this is where gradual exposure has an important place, perhaps trying them out during a role play session and with individuals you are confident with before going into public to practise them.

Alternative techniques are available to the cognitive therapist. One that seems particularly appropriate to blushing involves shifting people's focus of attention away from themselves. Self-consciousness is central to blushing; it is an anxious preoccupation with the self and a belief that you are the object of others' attention, that they are evaluating and judging you and that you are vulnerable to being criticised. Social skills training and mindfulness-based cognitive therapy are other available approaches.[14] Robert Edelmann provides a valuable introduction to fear of blushing and explains various psychological strategies and techniques to help people overcome their fears.[30]

A second key assumption of cognitive behaviour therapy is that therapies should be evaluated systematically and recommended on the basis of sound scientific evidence. In line with best practice in clinical research, the preference is for double-blind random control trials. The treatment under consideration is compared with alternative treatments or with a control group that receives no treatment. (This can be a 'waiting list' group who will eventually receive the treatment if it proves effective or, in drugs trials, a placebo-control group that receives a placebo rather than medication.) These alternative treatments form the conditions of the study. Participants are assigned to conditions at random. In 'blind' versions of trials the participants, researchers and those evaluating the treatments are unaware which individuals have been assigned to which condition.

There have been many randomised control trials of forms of cognitive behaviour therapy for social anxiety disorder and these have reported success in reducing anxieties.[13,14] There have been few studies specifically targeted at anxiety about blushing yet these too report success. For example, a randomised control trial conducted by Bögels compared the effectiveness of task concentration and relaxation training in conjunction with cognitive therapy in treatment for patients with social anxiety disorder.[3] The rationale for systematically practising task concentration as opposed to self-concentration is based on research that shows the close connection between blushing and self-focused attention. Cognitive therapy targeted participants' beliefs about their blushing, such as, "If I blush, everybody will find me weak". The study found that a combination treatment of task concentration and cognitive therapy was the most effective intervention for reducing fear of blushing.

Few randomised control trial studies have applied cognitive interventions for fear of blushing but this seems a promising approach given research that shows the effectiveness of this approach for social anxiety disorder. Not surprisingly, there are considerable similarities in the cognitions and safety behaviours between blushing anxiety and social anxiety and psychological interventions that pay sufficient attention to clients' beliefs about the specific nature of their problem are likely to be successful.

Beliefs about the causes and consequences of blushing, fear of doing so, and the bodily experience of blushing are inevitably closely intertwined, particularly if we take into account evidence that blushing is uncontrollable, that thinking about blushing can trigger one, and that focusing attention on the self is central to the blush and to feelings of anxiety more generally. Targeting beliefs seems a good place to start to help people overcome their distress.

Medication

Medication is a common form of treatment for social anxiety disorder, as it is for other anxiety disorders and depression. Four classes of drugs have been investigated for their application to the treatment of social anxiety disorder. These are drugs that have been developed for the treatment of other conditions; no new drugs have been developed specifically for this condition.

Two classes of drugs were originally used in the treatment of depression, the SSRIs (Selective Serotonin Re-uptake Inhibitors and the MAOIs (Mono-Amine Oxidase Inhibitors) including the reversible form of MAOIs (RIMAs, which have less potential for serious side effects than the MAOIs). These drugs are not interchangeable in the course of treatment: Reversible MAOIs should not be taken alongside MAOIs or SSRIs and a period of time must elapse before switching from one to the other.

The other two classes of drugs, Beta-Blockers and the Benzodiazepines, have been widely applied to the treatment of anxiety disorders. All these drugs are prescription-only. The SSRIs and MAOIs have been studied in clinical trials of the treatment of social anxiety disorder, and the SSRIs have emerged as the preferred pharmaceutical treatment for the condition.

In Britain, the National Institute for Health and Clinical Excellence (NICE) provides guidance for the National Health Service in England and Wales on the promotion of good health and the prevention and treatment of ill health. Their brief includes making recommendations about the effectiveness and safety of existing and new medicines. NICE is currently (in 2011) in the process of preparing clinical guidelines for social anxiety disorder, acknowledging its prevalence in the population, its impact on people's lives, and the need to improve treatment. It issued a 'scope' document in 2011, indicating its approach to producing recommended guidelines for the treatment of the disorder.[56]

In the absence (at the time of writing this) of detailed guidelines for social anxiety disorder it is instructive to examine the guidelines that have been produced for the management of anxiety, covering the conditions of Panic Disorder and Generalised Anxiety Disorder in adults; these were published in 2004 and amended in 2007.[55] They recommend three types of treatment, which they list in order of the strength of the evidence for their long-term effectiveness. First in the list is cognitive behaviour therapy. Second is pharmacology, where they recommend SSRIs. Their advice on benzodiazepines was that they should only be used in the short term and should not be prescribed for the treatment of panic disorder. Finally, in third place they refer to guided self-help including the use of self-help workbooks based upon cognitive behaviour therapy, as well as access to support groups.

Discussion of pharmaceutical treatments is beyond the scope of this paper. There are key issues of establishing the correct level of dosage for each patient bearing in mind their overall health and medical history, the importance of keeping to the doctor's guidelines, particularly with regard to the simultaneous use of other medications, keeping to the correct regime and coming off medication, as well as the management of possible side effects.

The interested reader should consult further reading on pharmacological treatment.[13, 14, 41, 67] If you think that this form of treatment might be for you, you should consult your general practitioner (GP) or physician. It is absolutely essential that pharmaceutical treatments must not be attempted without appropriate supervision by a qualified medical practitioner.

There is a wider debate about reliance on pharmacology to treat psychological conditions. It is argued that while they may provide relief in helping to manage symptoms they do not deal with the underlying causes. As we have seen, the cognitive approach proposes that anxieties are learned behaviours that are maintained by self-defeating strategies such as safety behaviours. If these strategies can be replaced, it is claimed, this would obviate the need for medication.

In addition, the role of pharmaceutical companies in psychiatric research has been criticised. It is argued that companies aim to promote sales of existing products by extending their application to normal psychological traits, for example, shyness, that are not illnesses and that this has been aided by the construction of new psychiatric diagnostic categories, introducing conditions such as social anxiety disorder.[22,46] There has been a large increase in prescriptions of drugs for the treatment of depression (these have doubled over the period 1991 to 2000, to more than 20 million prescriptions a year in England). There has also been an extension of the application of antidepressant medication, particularly the SSRIs, to additional conditions including social anxiety disorder.[22] Pharmaceutical companies provide funding to support clinical research into the effectiveness of the medicines that they have developed at huge expense, and it is argued that there can be a conflict of interest here. Strong claims may be made about the effectiveness of medications on the basis of poor quality research and the failure to publish negative findings.[39]

Of course, blushing is not an illness; nevertheless anxieties about it can have a powerful impact on the blusher's life. I now turn to consider a different approach to treatment that targets the blush itself.

Surgery

A surgical procedure known as endoscopic thoracic sympathectomy (ETS) uses endoscopic techniques to divide the sympathetic chain where it overlies the second and third rib in the upper thoracic region. An endoscope is a thin, lighted flexible tube with a camera at the end. It is inserted into the chest through a small incision beneath the armpit, enabling the surgeon to identify and cut the appropriate sympathetic nerve. The operation is irreversible although a recent study has reported success in the treatment of anxiety about blushing by clipping the nerve rather than cutting it, so that it is possible to restore the chain.[33] ETS was originally applied in the treatment of excessive sweating (hyperhidrosis) but it was extended in Sweden to the treatment of patients who were anxious about their blushing.

Christopher Drott, Goran Claes and their colleagues reported positive findings from a study of 244 patients with severe blushing anxieties.[23] The average age of participants in their study was 34 years with a range from 15 to 67 years. Questionnaires were sent to the patients after surgery: the average time of follow-up was 8 months after surgery, with a range from 2 months to 29 months. The success rates were high: 96% of respondents reported a reduced rate in blushing and 80% reported improvement in the social difficulties that their blushing had caused. Only 2% regretted having undergone the operation.

Yet there has been concern about possible side effects of ETS over and above the normal risks associated with any major surgery, such as bleeding and infection and the procedure is now controversial.[25] The most common side effects mentioned by patients are compensatory sweating and 'gustatory' sweating associated with tastes and smells. Several web sites have been set up by patients and others who have been unhappy about, and sought treatment for their excessive sweating [patients against ETS; http://www.no-ets.com/sideeffects.html]. There are arguments that clinical studies have underestimated the degree of dissatisfaction and regret, and that side effects have appeared in the longer term and would not have been picked up in relatively short-term follow-up questionnaires.

Concerns have also been expressed about the appropriateness of such operations for younger people, given that adolescence is a peak time for self-consciousness and embarrassability as well as for blushing. Many patients, it is suggested, might 'grow out of' anxieties about their blushing, as social pressures upon them decline or they gain in confidence in the kinds of social situations that trigger a blush: for example, anxiety about dating might reduce when you enter a steady relationship.

Other adverse effects of ETS are rarer but they lead to problems in a minority of cases, for example a collapsed lung following surgery, the onset of Horner's syndrome (a droopy eyelid, constriction of the pupil and dryness of the affected side of the face) or Raynaud's phenomenon (narrowing of the arteries carrying blood to the skin, which results in reduced circulation to the hands, experienced as pins and needles and numbness and redness of the skin).

A review of research into ETS for the Finnish Office for Health Technology Assessment published in 2005[49] (and in a refereed academic journal in 2007[50]) concluded that the quality of much of the published research was poor – in particular they noted the absence of randomised control trials – and that there was insufficient attention to following up the participants for longer than two years. The review concluded (p. 6) that 'due to lack of controlled trials there is no reliable evidence for the effectiveness of endoscopic thoracic sympathectomy for excessive sweating in the face or hands or for flushing of the face. Neither is there any evidence that this treatment has an impact on social phobia. Endoscopic thoracic sympathectomy is associated with significant immediate and long-term adverse effects'.[49]

The procedure is based on the assumption that the reddening is at the heart of the blusher's anxieties and pays little attention to the possibility that these would remain after the surgery. This would be the case if the blush was a sign of social anxiety; in these circumstances interventions that targeted the anxiety would be recommended. It is conceivable that anxiety could be greater after the procedure if it meant that the individual remained anxious about social encounters but now did not have the blush to blame this on.

Answers to these questions require long-term follow-up of patients who have undergone alternative forms of treatment. However, it would not be ethical to conduct a randomised control trial given the uncertainties about the surgical procedure and its effects so even then the outcomes might be difficult to interpret (different patients might be attracted to different treatments so might not be equivalent in terms of level or form of anxiety or other relevant factors to start with).

Conclusions

Let us return to the questions we posed at the beginning. What is a blush? And why do we do it? Does everybody blush, whatever their complexion? Do some people do it more than others, women more than men, perhaps, or younger more than older people? Do young children blush? Why do many people find blushing such an unpleasant experience?

What is a blush? As the research I have reported shows, there is no short answer to these questions. The blush is produced by vasodilation of blood vessels in the 'blush region' leading to increased blood flow just below the skin in this region. The system of blood vessels in this region is distinctive, with a high density of blood vessels close to the skin surface and the ability to move blood quickly to the facial skin area. These vessels play a part in thermoregulation; sympathetically controlled constriction of vessels decreases blood flow to the skin and helps heat retention in cold conditions.

Sympathetic nervous system activity producing relaxation of constriction increases blood flow close to the skin in order to reduce body heat in hot conditions, but although this process results in reddening of the face it does not seem sufficient to produce a blush. Rather, the available evidence suggests that in the blush increased blood flow is triggered by sympathetic nervous system activity acting upon beta-adrenergic receptors in the veins to produce dilation. Blushing can be prevented by cutting or clipping the sympathetic nerves that supply the blood vessels of the face, as demonstrated in the surgical process of endoscopic thoracic sympathectomy. It can be reduced by administration of drugs antagonistic to sympathetic activity. There may be involvement of local regulatory mechanisms and hormones circulating in the blood in addition to neural processes; as yet, the mechanisms involved in blushing are not fully understood.

Why do we blush? Psychophysiological research is beginning to add to our knowledge of the mechanisms involved in the blush. A more challenging question is why this process is triggered in certain kinds of circumstances, apparently across all the peoples of the world whatever their skin complexion, yet only in our species. The kinds of situations are essentially social, involving interactions with others. (We may blush when alone, but only when recalling a social event; it is not clear whether imagining an event can also do so.) It is not just any kind of social event (although some people claim to blush almost anywhere) and there have been attempts to characterise these.

The most commonly proposed circumstances are those that give rise to the experience of shame, embarrassment and shyness. All of these involve self-consciousness, the awareness of being the object of social attention. This raises further questions. Does the blush accompany all circumstances of shame, embarrassment and shyness, or only some of these? And if the latter, what is distinctive about these? Is it awareness of all kinds of attention from others, or only unwanted attention? In any case, why should our reaction to being the object of attention take this particular form? A number of answers have been put forward.

(i) The blush is a direct response to attention. This was Darwin's proposal. We blush when we believe we are the object of the attention of others; we blush on the face because this is the part of us that attracts most attention, and attention has a direct vasodilation effect on blood vessels. Darwin's emphasis on the blusher believing her- or himself to be the object of attention has been influential, but the specific mechanism he proposed has attracted little research interest. However, as we have seen, there appears to be supportive evidence from the findings reported by Drummond and Mirco that found increased blood flow on the side of the forehead that is being scrutinised by an observer but no change in blood flow on the non-scrutinised side. This finding, perhaps the most intriguing in recent research into blushing, deserves to be followed up.

(ii) The blush functions as a signal. This explanation was explicitly rejected by Darwin but it is the one that subsequently has attracted the most research interest. The economist Frank regarded the blush as a socially useful indication of honesty and trustworthiness, the more so as it is beyond the blusher's control and cannot be faked. Other approaches to understanding the blush as a signal look for similar functions across species. Visual displays that include colour changes are evident in non-human species, particularly in sexual selection where, usually, males make displays of their strength to potential mates or where females indicate their sexual availability. Signals that are 'honest' can have costs, on the basis that the ability to withstand the costs is itself an indication of the signaller's strength, as in the peacock display. The blush might have its origins in sexual displays. There is a close relation between sexual behaviour and the blush, as Darwin observed; however, as we have argued, this is a complex relation in humans.

Non-human animals that live together in groups have ways of communicating dominance and submission relations and these might have their counterpart in human social life. The blush has been thought of as a sign of appeasement, of apology, of placation[37], and of remediation[21]. Appeasement implies submissiveness, a power differential, acting to placate someone by giving in to their demands. An apology is an acknowledgement of wrongdoing and an admission of regret. Placation is the attempt to reduce someone's anger.

Castelfranchi and Poggi provide a thorough analysis of the blush in these terms: 'an acknowledgement, a confession, and an apology aimed at inhibiting the others' aggression or avoiding social ostracism'.[8] A series of studies has researched this proposal, and findings do support the hypothesis that observers judge actors less negatively if the actor is seen to blush after committing a wrongdoing. Blushing actors are not always viewed more positively, and how they are viewed depends on the context. This is not inconsistent with the notion that the blush serves as a signal, since signals are context-dependent.

The principal problem with the signal explanation is that the blush is less visible in large numbers of people in the world, depending on their skin pigmentation, even though the experience of the blush seems to be universal. A blush does convey information to the blusher himself or herself, and this may serve as a signal to the self, perhaps as a warning: the comedian and writer Andy Hamilton suggested to me that it might be equivalent to the yellow card that the referee shows to a footballer after a misdemeanour to indicate to the player and to everyone else that the next serious offence would result in the player being expelled from the game. For people with a paler complexion, and hence a more visible reddening, the warning would receive additional impetus from their awareness through experience that the blush is visible to others. This shows others that we are discomfited and that the matter that gives rise to a warning may become known.

(iii)The blush is an expression of emotion. Facial expressions of emotion are not restricted to humans and many human expressions can be universally recognised across the world. What emotion is expressed by the blush? The most common answer is embarrassment and there is no doubt that a blush frequently accompanies feelings of embarrassment. Whether it always does and whether it accompanies other emotions as well are issues that are unresolved. The blush is produced by activity of the sympathetic nervous system which is heavily involved in emotional experience and bodily changes, for example the changes that occur in fear, anxiety and anger. Some emotion theorists regard embarrassment as a form of anxiety but the blush does not seem to be a typical expression of fear or anxiety which are more likely to find expression in facial pallor, as blood is diverted to the musculature in preparation for fight or flight response.

Shame is also associated with the blush, particularly in older accounts, although some recent theorists, for example, as we have seen, Castelfranchi and Poggi refer in their account to shame rather than to embarrassment. The relation between these two emotions is controversial. Do they differ only in degree, in that shame is a more intense or serious form of embarrassment? Or are they qualitatively different? For example, humour frequently accompanies embarrassment but is rarely associated with shame and seems out of place there.

An alternative explanation is to regard a facial flush as an element in an undifferentiated arousal reaction, perhaps triggered by awareness that you are the object of attention, and this is interpreted as a blush depending on the circumstances of the situation, the context, or how you feel about yourself in the situation. Research in the social psychology of emotion has conducted experiments where people are encouraged through the alternative descriptions of the event to interpret their physiological reaction to the event in different ways. For example, participants might be encouraged to believe that their reaction, say of feeling hot, is due either to themselves ('this is an embarrassing situation') or to the environment ('the room is very hot') in order to investigate how the participants' emotional experience is influenced by the attribution they make about the causes of their experience of bodily changes.

A blush might operate in this way. However, empirical studies which conclude that increases in skin conductance measures (which are typically regarded as an index of general arousal) are uncorrelated with increases in measures of blood flow and cheek temperature taken during blush-eliciting circumstances would not support this conjecture.[63]

An alternative to this version of an arousal theory is that the blush is not the product of an increase in arousal but is brought about by the interruption of an increase in arousal that has already started. As we have seen, an explanation along these lines has been proffered by Frijda[35] and Salzen[62]. This might help explain the connection between the blush and embarrassment since the latter functions as a 'barrier' or 'stop' in a social encounter: we are uncertain how to proceed and are flustered because of this. It is consistent with the exposure account of the blush since sudden exposure of the self might also result in interruption of ongoing activity, as if we were 'trapped in the headlights' of public attention.

To summarise, there are several competing hypotheses about why certain kinds of social circumstances trigger – apparently automatically – a process of vasodilation of blood vessels in the facial area producing colour and temperature changes.

Individual differences. Darwin proposed that women blush more than men, but research has not found consistent support for this proposition. As I have argued above, I think that this is a more difficult question than first meets the eye and that the evidence we have does not do justice to this complexity. Most of us blush only in certain circumstances and this needs to be taken into account when estimating variation in the relative frequency with which people blush. Certainly, sexual topics and bodily exposure represent a frequent source of blushing and this may impact upon gender differences in propensity to blush. Closer analysis might tease out whether sexual topics and activities are inherently blush-making or whether this relation is more to do with culturally relative norms and values about sexuality and the meanings it has for individuals and for societies.

It does seem that blushing is at a peak during adolescence and early adulthood and decreases with age. Again, this needs further investigation. Is this a reliable finding and can it be obtained in different cultures? Is it a question of the kinds of situations we are likely to encounter at different stages of our life, and hence their tendency to elicit self-consciousness, are there physiological factors influencing vasodilation mechanisms as we grow older, or are both processes at work?

What is more certain is that we know very little about the emergence of the blush in childhood and the factors that influence its emergence. We have extensive evidence of the development of self-awareness, shyness and embarrassment and this research needs to be joined up with the study of the blush.

Anxiety about blushing. Shame is an extremely unpleasant experience and feelings of shyness and embarrassment can be more or less pleasant depending on the context and the individual's view of himself or herself. The experience of intense embarrassment may be as disagreeable as the experience of shame. The unwanted exposure of something about ourselves is also unpleasant and to be feared.

Since the blush often accompanies these experiences and provides a signal to the blusher and, as he or she might believe, to others as well, that he or she is faced with these difficulties, it is not surprising that many people are anxious about their blushing and take steps, perhaps extreme steps, to avoid or cope with it. Fear of blushing is commonly associated with social anxiety. Like anxiety it can vary from mild discomfort that we can cope with to experiences that have a marked impact on the quality of our life, restricting our social life and creating worry and depression. People who meet the diagnostic criteria for social anxiety disorder report anxieties about blushing.

Research studies that distinguish people diagnosed with social anxiety disorder who either have or do not have specific concerns about their blushing are helping us to understand the relative contributions of the facts of blushing and their subjective experience. In reality these are closely linked, but evidence suggests that psychological interventions targeted at changing subjective beliefs seem to provide a promising approach to help people cope with their anxieties including blushing concerns. Nevertheless, we do need more controlled studies to investigate the long term benefits of psychological therapies targeted at blushing concerns.

In conclusion. The blush is a fascinating phenomenon that we are only beginning to understand. In this book I have examined some of its causes, both psychological and physiological, and have considered its potential consequences for the person who blushes and for others who are present at the time. A blush may be fleeting and not necessarily noticed by those who are present yet it is not a negligible phenomenon: it contributes in many ways to our social life and to our sense of who we are. I hope that this publication has whetted your appetite to learn more about blushing and about embarrassment, shyness and anxiety. If you are anxious about your blushing I hope too that you have learned something about its nature, understand that you are not alone in having these concerns, and have acquired some useful information about where you might find help to overcome your anxieties.

References

1. Ayers, B. N., Forshaw, M. J., & Hunter, M. S. (2011). The menopause. *The Psychologist*, 24, 348-352.

2. Bergmann, M. S. (2004). *Understanding Dissonance and Controversy in the History of Psychoanalysis*. New York: Other Press LLC.

3. Bögels, S. M. (2006). Task concentration training versus applied relaxation, in combination with cognitive therapy, for social phobia patients with fear of blushing, trembling, and sweating. *Behaviour Research and Therapy*, 44, 1199-1210.

4. Bögels, S. M., & Reith, W. (1999). Validity of two questionnaires to assess social fears: The Dutch Social Phobia and Anxiety Inventory and the Blushing, Trembling, and Sweating Questionnaire. *Journal of Psychopathology and Behavioral Assessment*, 21, 51-66.

5. Burgess, T. H. (1839). *The Physiology or Mechanism of Blushing*. London: John Churchill. Reprinted by BiblioLife, Charleston, SC, 2009.

6. Buss, A. H., Iscoe, I., & Buss, E. H. (1979). The development of embarrassment. *Journal of Psychology*, 103, 227-230.

7. Casimir M. J., & Schnegg M. (2002). Shame across cultures: the evolution, ontogeny and

function of a 'moral emotion'. In H. Keller, Y. H. Poortinga, & A. Schölmerich (Eds.), *Between Culture and Biology: Perspectives on Ontogenetic Development*. Cambridge: Cambridge University Press, 270-300.

8. Castelfranchi C., & Poggi I. (1990). Blushing as a discourse: Was Darwin wrong? In W. R. Crozier (Ed.), *Shyness and Embarrassment: Perspectives from Social Psychology*. New York: Cambridge University Press, 230-251.

9. Cockburn, C., & Clarke, G. (2002). "Everybody's looking at you!": Girls negotiating the "femininity deficit" they incur in physical education. *Women's Studies International Forum*, 25, 651-665.

10. Crozier, W. R. (2000). Blushing, social anxiety, and exposure. In W. R. Crozier (Ed.), *Shyness: Development, Consolidation and Change*. London: Routledge, 154-170.

11. Crozier, W. R. (2001). Blushing and the exposed self: Darwin revisited. *Journal for the Theory of Social Behaviour*, 31, 61-72.

12. Crozier, W. R. (2006). *Blushing and the Social Emotions*. Basingstoke: Palgrave Macmillan.

13. Crozier, W. R., & Alden, L. E. (Eds.) (2005). *International Handbook of Social Anxiety for Clinicians*. Chichester, Sussex: John Wiley.

14. Crozier, W. R. & Alden, L. E. (2009). *Coping with Shyness and Social Phobia.* Oxford: Oneworld.

15. Darwin, C. (1872/1999). *The Expression of the Emotions in Man and Animals.* First published in 1872. Corrected third edition with an introduction, afterword, and commentaries by Paul Ekman, published 1999. London: HarperCollins.

16. de Jong, P. J. (1999). Communicative and remedial effects of social blushing. *Journal of Nonverbal Behavior,* 23, 197-217.

17. de Jong, P. J., & Peters, M. L. (2005). Do blushing phobics overestimate the undesirable effects of their blushing? *Behavioural Research and Therapy,* 43, 747-758.

18. de Jong, P. J., Peters, M. L., & De Cremer, D. (2003). Blushing may signify guilt: Revealing effects of blushing in ambiguous situations. *Motivation and Emotion*, 27, 225-249.

19. de Jong, P. J., Peters, M. L., De Cremer, D., & Vranken, C. (2002). Blushing after a moral transgression in a prisoner's dilemma game: Appeasing or revealing? *European Journal of Social Psychology*, 32, 627-644.

20. Dijk, C., de Jong, P. J, Müller, E., & Boersma, W. (2010). Blushing-fearful individuals' judgmental biases and conditional beliefs: An internet inquiry. *Journal of*

Psychopathology and Behavioral Assessment, 32, 264–270.

21. Dijk, C., de Jong, P. J., & Peters, M. L. (2009). The remedial value of blushing in the context of transgressions and mishaps. *Emotion,* 9, 287-291.

22. Double, D. (2002). The limits of psychiatry. *British Medical Journal,* 324 (7342), 900-904.

23. Drott, C., Claes G., & Rex L. (2002). Facial blushing treated by sympathetic denervation – longstanding benefits in 831 patients. *Journal of Cosmetic Dermatology,* 138, 639-43.

24. Drummond, P. D. (1997). The effect of adrenergic blockade on blushing and facial flushing. *Psychobiology,* 34, 163-168.

25. Drummond, P. D. (2004). Endoscopic transthoracic sympathectomy for blushing. *Journal of Cosmetic Dermatology,* 2, 45.

26. Drummond, P. D., Back, K., Harrison, J., Helgadottir, F. D., Lange, B., Lee, C., Leavy, K., Novatscou, C., Orner, A., Pham, H., Prance, J., Radford, D., & Wheatley, L. (2007). Blushing during social interactions in people with a fear of blushing. *Behaviour Research and Therapy,* 45, 1601-1608.

27. Drummond, P. D., & Lim, H. K. (2000). The significance of blushing for fair-and dark-skinned people. *Personality and Individual Differences,* 29, 1123-1132.

28. Drummond, P. D., & Mirco, N. (2004). Staring at one side of the face increases blood flow on that side of the face. *Psychophysiology*, 41, 281-287.

29. Edelmann, R. J. (1990). Embarrassment and blushing: A component-process model, some initial descriptive and cross-cultural data. In W. R. Crozier (Ed.), *Shyness and Embarrassment: Perspectives from Social Psychology*. New York: Cambridge University Press, 205-229.

30. Edelmann, R. J. (2004). *Coping with Blushing*. London: Sheldon Press.

31. Fahlén, T. (1997). Core symptom patterns of social phobia. *Depression and Anxiety*, 4, 223-232.

32. Farooq, S., & Griggs, G. (2008). Girls from ethnic minorities: Participation in sport. *PE & Sport Today*, August. Available at http://www.teachingexpertise.com/articles/girls-ethnic-minorities-sports-participation-3991. Accessed 14th September 2011.

33. Fibia, J. F., Molins, L., Mier, J. M., & Vidal, G. (2009). Effectiveness of sympathetic block by clipping in the treatment of hyperhidrosis and facial blushing. *Interactive CardioVascular and Thoracic Surgery*, 9, 970-972.

34. Frank, R. H. (1988). *Passions within Reason: The Strategic Role of the Emotions*. New York: Norton.

35. Frijda, N. J. (1986). *The Emotions*. Cambridge: Cambridge University Press.

36. Gerlach, A. L., & Ultes, M. (2003). Übserschneidung von Socializer Phobie und ubermässigem Schwitzen und Erröten – eine internetbasierte Studie. In R. Ott & C. Eichenberg (Eds.), *Klinische Psychologie im Internet*, Göttingen: Horgrefe Verlag, 327-341.

37. Halberstadt, A. G., & Green, L. R. (1993). Social attention and placation theories of blushing. *Motivation and Emotion*, 17, 53-64.

38. Harré, R. (1990). Embarrassment: A conceptual analysis. In W. R. Crozier (Ed.), *Shyness and Embarrassment: Perspectives from Social Psychology*. New York: Cambridge University Press, 181-204.

39. Healy, D. (2006). *Let Them Eat Prozac: The Unhealthy Relationship Between the Pharmaceutical Industry and Depression*. New York: New York University Press.

40. Henderson, L., & Zimbardo, P. G. (2001). Shyness, social anxiety, and social phobia. In S. G. Hofmann & P. M. DiBartolo (Eds.), *From Social Anxiety to Social Phobia: Multiple Perspectives*. Needham Heights, MA: Allyn & Bacon, 46-64.

41. Hood, S. D., & Nutt, D. J. (2005). Psychopharmacological treatments: An overview, in W. R. Crozier & L. E. Alden (Eds.), *The Essential Handbook of Social Anxiety for Clinicians*. Chichester, Sussex: Wiley, 287-320.

42. Jablonski, N. G. (2006). *Skin: A Natural History*. Berkeley: University of California Press.

43. Karch, F. E. (1971). Blushing. *Psychoanalytic Review*, 58, 37-50.

44. Keltner, D. (1995). Signs of appeasement: Evidence for the distinct displays of embarrassment, amusement, and shame. *Journal of Personality and Social Psychology*, 68, 441-454.

45. Keltner, D., & Buswell, B. N. (1997). Embarrassment: Its distinct form and appeasement functions. *Psychological Bulletin*, 122, 250-70.

46. Lane, C. (2007). *Shyness: How Normal Behavior Became a Sickness*. New Haven: Yale University Press.

47. Leary, M. R., Britt, T. W., Cutlip, W. D., & Templeton, J. L. (1992). Social blushing. *Psychological Bulletin*, 107, 446-460.

48. Lewis, M., Sullivan, M. W., Stanger, C., & Weiss, M. (1989). Self-development and self-conscious emotions. *Child Development*, 60, 146-156.

49. Malmivaara, A., Kuukasjärvi, P., Autti-Rämö, I., Kovanen, N., & Mäkelä, M. (2005). *Effectiveness and safety of endoscopic thoracic sympathectomy: A systematic review*. FinOHTA Report 26/2005. Helsinki: Finnish Office for Health Assessment FinOHTA/National Research and Development Centre for Welfare

and Health STAKES. Available at http://www.stakes.fi/finohta/ Accessed 31 August 2011 [Paper in Finnish; Abstract in English]

50. Malmivaara, A., Kuukasjärvi, P., Autti-Rämö, I., Kovanen, N., & Mäkelä, M. (2007). Effectiveness and safety of endoscopic thoracic sympathectomy for excessive sweating and facial blushing: A systematic review. *International Journal of Technology Assessment in Health Care*, 23, 54-62.

51. Maynard Smith, J., & Harper, D. (2003). *Animal Signals*. Oxford: Oxford University Press.

52. Mellander, S., Andersson, P.O., Afzelius, L.E., & Hellstrand, P. (1982). Neural beta adrenergic dilatation of the facial vein in man. Possible mechanism in emotional blushing. *Acta Physiologica Scandinavica* 114, 393-399.

53. Miller, R. S. (1996). *Embarrassment: Poise and Peril in Everyday Life*. New York: Guilford Press.

54. Mulkens, S., de Jong, P. J., Dobbelaar, A., & Bögels, S. M. (1999). Fear of blushing: Fearful preoccupation irrespective of facial coloration. *Behaviour Research and Therapy*, 37, 1119-1128.

55. National Institute for Health and Clinical Excellence (2007). *Quick Reference Guide (amended). Anxiety: managements of anxiety (Panic disorder, with or without agoraphobia,*

and generalised anxiety disorder) in adults in primary, secondary and community care. Clinical Guideline 22 (amended). London: National Institute for Clinical Excellence. http://www.nice.org.uk/CG022

56. National Institute for Clinical Excellence (2011). *Social Anxiety Disorder: Final Scope* June 10th 2011. http://www.nice.org.uk/nicemedia/live/12950/54 822/54822.pdf. Accessed 19th August 2011.

57. No Panic. http://www.nopanic.org.uk/ Accessed 16th January 2012.

58. Nordin, M. (1990). Sympathetic discharges in the supraorbital nerve and their relation to sudo- and vasomotor responses. *Journal of Physiology*, 423, 241-255.

59. Öhman, A. (2005). The role of the amygdala in human fear: Automatic detection of threat. *Psychoneuroendocrinology*, 30, 953-958.

60. Rouf, K., Fennell, M., Westbrook, D., Cooper, M., & Bennett-Levy, J. (2004). Devising effective behavioural experiments. In J. Bennett-Levy, G. Butler, M. Fennell, A. Hackmann, M. Mueller, & D. Westbrook (Eds.), *Oxford Guide to Behavioural Experiments*. Oxford: Oxford University Press, 21-58.

61. Sabini, J., Siepmann, M., Stein, J., & Meyerowitz (2000). Who is embarrassed by what? *Cognition and Emotion*, 14, 213-240

62. Salzen, E. (2010). Letter: Flushing and blushing. *The Psychologist*, 23, 539.

63. Schoenfeldt, M. (2004). "Commotion Strange": Passion in *Paradise Lost*, in G. K. Paster, K. Rowe, & M. Floyd-Wilson (Eds.), *Reading the Early Passions: Essays in the Critical History of Emotion.* Philadelphia: University of Pennsylvania Press, 43-67.

64. Shearn, D., Spellman, L., Straley, B., Meirick, J., & Styker, K. (1999). Empathic blushing in friends and strangers. *Motivation and Emotion,* 23, 307-316.

65. Shields, S. A., Mallory, M. E., & Simon, A. (1990). The experience and symptoms of blushing as a function of age and reported frequency of blushing. *Journal of Nonverbal Behavior,* 14, 171-187.

66. Sievert, L. L., & Flanagan, E. K. (2005). Geographical distribution of hot flash frequencies: Considering climatic influences. *American Journal of Physical Anthropology,* 128, 437-443.

67. Simon, A., & Shields, S. A. (1996). Does complexion color affect the experience of blushing? *Journal of Social Behavior and Personality,* 11, 177-188.

68. Social Anxiety UK. http://www.social-anxiety.org.uk/ Accessed 6th February 2012.

69. Strathern, A. (1977). Why is shame on the skin? In J. Blacking (Ed.), *The Anthropology of the Body.* London: Academic Press, 99-110.

70. Witkin, J. K. (1988). Why is flushing limited to a mostly facial cutaneous distribution?

Journal of the American Academy of Dermatology, 19, 309-31.

71. Voncken, M. J., & Bögels, S. M. (2009). Physiological blushing in social anxiety disorder patients with and without blushing complaints: Two subtypes? *Biological Psychology*, 81, 86-94.

72. Zahavi, A. (1975). Mate selection – A selection for a handicap. *Journal of Theoretical Biology*, 53, 205-214.

Further reading

For a book-length overview of psychological research into the blush, see my book, *Blushing and the Social Emotions*, published by Palgrave Macmillan in 2006. The book includes chapters on the nature of the blush, its physiology and causes. It discusses the relation of blushing to embarrassment, shame, shyness, guilt and anger. Finally, it discusses individual differences in tendency to blush, anxieties about blushing, and interventions to help people overcome their anxieties.

I also discuss blushing in my overview of research into shyness: *Understanding Shyness: Psychological Perspectives*, published by Palgrave Macmillan in 2001 and available as a paperback

Peter de Jong and I have edited a book comprising a set of original chapters on blushing: *The Psychological Significance of the Blush*, due to be published by Cambridge University Press in December 2012. It features original chapters written for it by many of the researchers whose work I discuss in this book as well as by other leading researchers into embarrassment, shyness, social anxiety and ethology. It covers the measurement of blushing, clinical interventions for fear of blushing, rosacea, psychological theories of blushing and embarrassment, the blush as a signal, and the parts played by colour changes as signals in other species. I will update information about this publication as it becomes available. See also my web site, www.raycrozier.com.

Robert J. Edelmann's *Coping with Blushing* (Sheldon Press, 2004) offers a short, readable yet thorough account of blushing and provides a very helpful description of how fear of blushing may be overcome using cognitive therapy and relaxation techniques. Professor Edelmann contributed a chapter on blushing to *The International Handbook of Social Anxiety* edited by Lynn E. Alden and myself and published by Wiley in 2001.

Coping with Shyness and Social Phobia, a book that I co-authored with Lynn Alden (Oneworld Publications, 2009) provides a clearly written overview of psychological and pharmaceutical interventions for helping people overcome shyness and for the treatment of social anxiety disorder. It includes a chapter on coping with blushing. This book is available in paperback and is aimed at anyone who would like to learn more about social anxiety and its treatment. Longer and more technical books on social anxiety are the collections of original chapters written by leading international researchers and clinicians edited by Lynn Alden and myself: *The International Handbook of Social Anxiety,* mentioned above, and *The Essential Handbook of Social Anxiety for Clinicians* (published by Wiley, 2005). The latter book comprises an updated selection of the more clinically oriented chapters from the first book, and is available as a paperback and as a Kindle eBook. Another valuable source on the meaning of social anxiety disorder and the rationale and effectiveness of psychological and pharmacological interventions is *Fearing Others*, by Ariel Stravynski (Cambridge University Press, 2007).

The Expression of the Emotions in Man and Animals by Charles Darwin is readily available on the Internet and an edition (free, as I write this) is published as a Kindle eBook. The annotated paperback edition prepared by Paul Ekman (see reference list) includes very interesting comments on research into emotional expression since Darwin's publication. Janet Browne provides a valuable account of the background to Darwin's chapter in her chapter in D. Kohn (ed.) *The Darwinian Heritage (*Princeton University Press, 1985). Chapter 5 in Thomas Dixon's *From Passions to Emotions* (Cambridge University Press, 2003) examines Darwin's theory in the context of arguments for design theology.

For further information on the psychology of fear and the amygdala and sub-cortical processing of threat stimuli, see Joseph LeDoux's classic book, *The Emotional Brain,* available in paperback published by Phoenix, 2004. See also his web site: www.cns.nyu.edu/home/ledoux/

The textbook *Cardiovascular Physiology Concepts* by Richard E. Klabunde (Lippincott, Williams & Wilkins, 2005) provides a detailed technical account of the mechanisms involved in the vasodilation of blood vessels.

The Principles of Psychology by William James, first published in 1890 by Henry Holt, New York, is available as a Kindle eBook.

The novel *Daniel Deronda* by George Eliot is available in several editions. My quotation describing circumstances where a character blushes when she believes that her thoughts are revealed can be found on page 416 of the Penguin Classics Edition, published by Penguin Books, 1967.

The author

Raymond Crozier BA (Hons.) MSc Ph.D. C.Psychol. FBPsS was formerly Professor of Psychology in the School of Social Sciences, Cardiff University, UK, and Professor of Psychology and Programme Director of the undergraduate degree in Psychosocial Sciences in the University of East Anglia, UK. Currently he is Honorary Professor at Cardiff University and Visiting Fellow at the University of East Anglia. He is a Chartered Psychologist and an elected Fellow of The British Psychological Society. He has published extensively on shyness, shame and blushing; the psychology of education; the psychology of art and design. He has appeared on numerous local, national and international radio and television programmes. In addition to the books listed in this publication, he has published, among others:

Individual Learners: Personality Differences in Education (Routledge, 1997); translated into Spanish by Pablo Manzano as *Diferencias Individuales en el Apprehendizaje* (Madrid: Narcea).

Manufactured Pleasures: Psychological Responses to Design (Manchester University Press, 1994); translated by Farkas Andras into Hungarian as: *Pszichologia es Design* (Budapest: Nemzeti Tankonyvkiado).

Understanding Shyness: Psychological Perspectives (Palgrave, 2001); translated into Chinese simplified characters by Wang Bing (Beijing, China: SDX Publishing Company, 2004); translated into Arabic (Safat, Kuwait: National Council for Culture, Arts & Letters, 2009).

(with Antony J. Chapman, co-editor), *Cognitive Processes in the Perception of Art* (Amsterdam, North-Holland, 1984).

(editor), *Shyness and Embarrassment: Perspectives from Social Psychology* (Cambridge University Press, 1990).

(with Robert H. Ranyard and Ola Svenson, co-editors) *Decision Making: Cognitive Models and Explanations* (Routledge, 1997).

(with Lynn E. Alden, co-editor) *International Handbook of Social Anxiety* (Wiley, 2001)

(with Peter J. de Jong, co-editor) *The Psychological Significance of the Blush* (Cambridge University Press, in press)

Visit my web site at www.raycrozier.com for further details.

www.ingramcontent.com/pod-product-compliance
Lightning Source LLC
Chambersburg PA
CBHW072328290526
45794CB00002B/788